I speak at dozens of events a year and I know what a difference professionalism makes. Sasha Frieze is the guru of business events and the advice you ~~~d is right here.

Finkelstein,
ist, *The Times*

Having spoken　　　　　　　　　　　　　decades, I've
witnessed firstha　　　　　　　　　　　　)eriences that
deliver genuine i

As a CMO, I recognize that events are increasingly a critical component of organizational success, and *The Chief Event Officer's Playbook* provides exactly what leaders need – packed with clear thinking and deep insights to help achieve this impact. This must-read book offers a practical framework for placing events at the heart of your brand, culture and strategy, ultimately helping to power your organization's success.

Laurent Ezekiel,
Chief Marketing Officer, WPP and CEO, WPP Open X

This brilliant book provides an invaluable event blueprint for any business leader. As someone who has advised numerous organizations on strategy, I understand the crucial role events play in bringing purpose to life. In an AI-first world, in-person events will become increasingly significant – one of the few genuinely trustworthy marketing channels remaining.

The strategic frameworks, especially the Event Purpose Proposition, provide clarity and empower organizations, from the CEO to executives at all levels, to clearly articulate their event's strategic purpose and ensure every event is impactful and aligned with broader goals.

Piers Linney,
Former Dragons' Den Investor, Co-founder, Implement AI

A superbly written how-to guide from one of the best in the business.

Nick Wallis,
Author and speaker

Our business is built upon developing brands on the back of live experiences. *The Chief Event Officer's Playbook* gives language to what works. We've trusted Sasha Frieze to advise our teams and this book distils sharp insight into deep strategy. It's a book that is built for decision-makers who need events to drive results, not just attendance.

Gareth Bowhill,
CEO, CloserStill Media

Events have always been a core sector of the Experience Economy, and in *The Chief Event Officer's Playbook* Sasha Frieze shows you how to design events that are not only memorable but truly transformative. She recognizes that events have the power to change people and shows you how to create a Transformation Journey Plan that turns your attendees -- make that *participants* -- into the hero of your events.

B. Joseph Pine II,
Author, *The Experience Economy and The Transformation Economy: Guiding Customers to Achieve their Aspirations*

Sasha's essential event strategy toolkit is a must-read for everyone who understands the power of a game-changing gathering. She shares her unique formula for a successful programme, along with insider insights from other big names in the business.

Zoe Kleinman,
Technology Editor, BBC

Businesses care deeply about attention, trust, and brand authenticity – and events play a key role in all three. Sasha Frieze understands this. *The Chief Event Officer's Playbook* shows how events can be powerful strategic tools. It's a clear, insightful read for any leader wanting to align events with their business goals.

Tim Weller,
Media Entrepreneur, Founder Incisive Media,
Non-Executive Chairman

If you spend the time, money, and energy on an event, it should be transformative for participants to ensure the return on experience is high for everyone. *The Chief Event Officer's Playbook* shows organizations and event planners exactly how to design and execute extraordinary experiences that create powerful emotional responses that lead to transformation. Every event professional should read this book.

Paul J. Zak PhD,
Author of *The Little Book of Happiness: A Scientific Approach to Living Better*

What a great read! Sasha has blended her own wealth of experience with the most up to date insights, research, and trends from industry and thought leaders. Sprinkled throughout are relevant stories from her own personal and professional life. Don't just read this book, apply it and you will up your event creation game.

Mat Duerden,
Professor, Marriott School of Business, Brigham Young University

The Chief Event Officer's Playbook is packed with real, relatable examples and blends strategy with heart. As a fan of Simon Sinek's *Start with Why*, I love how it weaves personal insight with contemporary experience from the industry to create a grounded, purpose-first approach. Actionable and authentic, it is a must-read for the modern-day event planner. It's not just practical, it's transformational.

Shonali Devereux,
CEO, Meetings Industry Association

Sasha Frieze has for many years argued that events should sit at the heart of an organization. This book highlights why events are so much more than 'nice to haves.' Essential reading for anyone serious about the role events can play in shaping their sector.

Sir Nigel Shadbolt,
Principal Jesus College, Oxford

Events are the most important channel for marketing teams who rely on their Chief Event Officers to deliver events with genuine strategic purpose; delivering the bigger corporate strategy. Sasha's decades of experience and guidance in this book is an invaluable tool for senior event professionals and CMOs to ensure that their events deliver.

Anita Howard,
Founder, ICE, International Corporate Event
Awards and Network

Whether you are a Chief Event Officer, aspire to be one, or are an experience builder who is curious about designing transformative events, this playbook is an essential guide.

Packed with practical frameworks and templates to guide strategic decision-making at any stage of the process, Sasha cuts through the fluff to deliver direct insights and action steps, helping you to navigate our ever-changing industry with clarity, confidence and speed.

Naomi Clare Crellin,
Founder and CEO, Storycraft Lab

Having directed flagship global sponsorships – from the Premier League to Reading & Leeds Music Festivals – and grown two data businesses to successful exits, I know the difference between logistical noise and strategic impact.

In *The Chief Event Officer's Playbook*, Sasha Frieze distils decades of insight into a concise, actionable blueprint that elevates events from cost line to board-level catalyst. Her four-question framework and 5Cs model hand leaders a clear path to transformational, community-driven gatherings. Essential reading for anyone serious about turning meetings into momentum.

Mike Flynn,
Edutero Chairman and Serial Entrepreneur

Sasha Frieze has spent over 30 years transforming events from routine gatherings into high-impact experiences that drive real change. In *The Chief Event Officer's Playbook: How to Create Transformational Events*, she distils a lifetime of expertise into a must-read guide for anyone who understands that events are more than logistics. They are powerful tools for influence, innovation, and business success.

With a rare blend of creative vision and commercial acumen, Sasha has helped top organizations, media brands, and nonprofits craft events that leave lasting impressions. Whether you're a seasoned event leader or just starting out, this book will challenge your thinking and elevate your approach. If you want to create events that truly matter, you need this playbook on your shelf.

David Adler,
Founder, BizBash

In her book *The Chief Event Officer's Playbook*, Sasha Frieze provides a clear framework showing why live events are no longer just a 'nice to have' or a side piece to marketing. Instead, they are essential for business leaders looking to push their strategy and agenda forward.

Nick Gold,
Managing Director, Speakers Corner

Sasha has captured exactly what senior leaders need to hear about events. *The Chief Event Officer's Playbook* reframes events from logistics to strategic assets – something the events industry has needed for years. It's clear, grounded, and genuinely useful.

If you're serious about creating events that deliver business impact, this is the guide. Sasha brings years of real experience and deep thinking to the table, and it shows. This isn't theory – it's a manual for doing events properly, with purpose at the core.

Adam Parry,
Editor, *Event Industry News*

Events are powerful drivers of customer and member engagement – but too often, they're reduced to a logistics checklist, rather than focusing on the event experience, community and outcomes. Events are complex productions that demand a combination of strategic leadership and marketing.

I loved this book – it's exactly what the events industry has been crying out for. It's not another 'how-to' guide or academic tome, it's a genuinely inspiring, easy-to-read Playbook that helps you think bigger and deliver events with real purpose.

Packed with practical insights and storytelling that sticks, it's a book you will keep coming back to when you want to create experiences that actually mean something.

The Chief Event Officer's Playbook is strategy-led, warm, and purpose-driven, and will become the bible for making your events more than just dates in a diary.

Gina Kay,
Marketing Manager, Mash Media – International Confex

From the opening words to the final call to action, this is a book that re-frames what it means to be successful in events. It challenges decades of preconceptions and provides new models for those with the ambition to make events really count – both strategically and specifically for the communities we gather.

As someone who grew up in the world of B2B events when the chasm between the commercial event producers and the associations and in-house organizers was huge, this book conjures up a world of memories, reminding me of how far the profession has evolved, and how much more we can achieve.

It provides both a blueprint and an exhortation for us to do just that – creating exceptional events with intent and impact. At its heart, it is a love letter to the power of in-person events. To their authenticity and the transformative impact when carefully curated content and the community for whom it was painstakingly designed, connects and crescendos into a celebration of a shared purpose.

Susanna Kempe,
CEO, Laidlaw Foundation

Today's environment calls for a new kind of leader – one who sees events as a brand platform, not just a function. In *The Chief Event Officer's Playbook*, Sasha Frieze offers a blueprint for creating the kind of transformative, connected experiences that inspire action.

Todd Unger,
Chief Experience Officer, American Medical Association
and author, *The 10-Second Customer Journey*

With misinformation and mistrust prevalent, many of us crave authentic human connections that in-person gatherings bring. Sasha reframes live business events as transformational, community experiences, not the old-fashioned product showcases of yesteryear.

Her book makes a compelling case for elevating event professionals to the C-suite and provides a strategic framework that will revolutionize your gathering. Through personal stories and real-world examples, she reveals how purpose-driven events create the sense of belonging participants crave.

It's a love letter to the profound human impact of masterfully crafted events. Essential reading for anyone serious about creating experiences that truly matter.

Tamar Beck,
CEO, Gleanin

The old events industry – cold coffee, stale speakers, staler rooms – still lingers.

Enter *The Chief Event Officer's Playbook*, a handbook for experience creators, strategists, content creators and influencers. Crafted to help you create intentional events that transform, engage and move people.

The Chief Event Officer's Playbook shows how experience drives business success, with trailblazing brands leading the way, and how events can learn from this.

Both a user guide and a warm embrace to the events industry, this is a compelling narrative that introduces the world of transformational events, and the power they have in modern business.

Alistair Turner,
Managing Director, Eight PR & Marketing

This book is bang on the money and all event leaders should own a copy.

Tackling topics that are easy to push into the future – next gen event goers, business events' essential need for community and connections, the aptly named event conundrum of infoxication –

which often fall into the 'too hard' box. It digs into the importance of measuring event impact, beyond financial impact.

And most importantly, this is a call to arms to put strategic event conversations where they belong: firmly in the boardroom.

Our industry moves fast – chasing growth, seeking innovative projects, or putting out the latest fire; this book is a much-needed firebreak.

A moment to stop, reflect, and reset your strategic direction. Don't wonder if it's for you, just read it, and you'll see it is.

Vanessa Lovatt,
Founder, Event Tech World and Event Sector Consultant

The Chief Event Officer's Playbook is an essential guide for leaders who want to move beyond logistics and deliver events with lasting impact. Sasha combines strategy, creativity and industry expertise to show how events can drive transformation, not just transactions.

A must-read for anyone serious about the power of experiential leadership.

Flavilla Fongang,
CEO and Founder of Black Rise

The *Chief Event Officer's Playbook* is an inspirational read and I thoroughly enjoyed the approachable style. The tangible examples are an absolute gold mine – I highly recommend this to everyone who wants to transform their events; from the most senior to the most junior.

Abi Cannons,
Senior Strategic Account Manager, Grip

This book urges all event leaders to adopt a strategic mindset. Only then can we elevate our role as a strategic business partner and earn a seat at the table, driving pipeline and revenue.

This is the only way to allow our team members to elevate themselves beyond logistics, the only way for our roles to prove their strategic impact to the business.

This book is a must-read for all event professionals who aspire to a leadership position and who seek more than checklists and room rate negotiations.

Liz Lathan,
Co-founder, Club Ichi

In a world of saturation, attention is the most valuable currency. That makes events uniquely powerful: one of the few remaining contexts where people show up on purpose. *The Chief Event Officer's Playbook* is an excellent guide to stop treating events like logistics exercises and start seeing them for what they are: live laboratories of human behaviour.

When you design with that mindset, you stop guessing what works. This book is an intelligent manifesto for making events feel less like broadcast, more like belonging, and for building shared momentum that lasts. *The Chief Event Officer's Playbook* helps you create events that earn memories and that stick.

Lea Karam,
Behavioural Scientist, Founder and CEO, Mindscope

In an increasingly AI-driven business environment, it takes a brave business leader to ignore the power of events.

Events are a crucial part of the marketing ecosystem – without meeting customers, suppliers, competitors, future employees (or employers) in the flesh, your brand will inevitably become faceless and potentially irrelevant.

In good times events highlight excellence – in bad times they can be the life raft that keep you afloat and visible. This well-timed book guides you to create events are stimulating, thought provoking and impactful. Ignore it at your peril.

James Hanbury,
Media entrepreneur and investor,
co-founder Incisive Media

The Chief Event Officer's Playbook is a timely and essential guide for anyone serious about transforming events into powerful strategic tools. It highlights the critical importance of designing events with intention, creativity and a deep understanding of how people learn and engage.

In today's knowledge-driven economy, meetings and events are not just gatherings – they are catalysts for innovation and economic acceleration. This book offers a roadmap to creating impact through professional event design. Every page offers insight, every paragraph fuels inspiration. It's not just a book, it's a blueprint. I'm certain it will become the go-to bible for every forward-thinking event professional.

Linda Pereira,
CEO, CPL Events & Consultancy

With the rise of AI and changes in marketing, events have emerged as the most powerful channel – no longer optional, but a critical, strategic business function.

For years, event professionals have pushed to shed the party planner label and claim their rightful place at the heart of organizational strategy. This book gives you the blueprint to make that happen. Every event professional should read it – and so should every C-suite leader serious about the critical role of events in delivering on your big strategic objectives.

Will Curran,
Event industry influencer and successful
event agency owner

This book captures the true alchemy of transformational events. By distilling the essence of gatherings into the 5Cs: Content, Connection, Celebration, Community and Ceremony, it provides a clear and compelling framework for anyone who wants to design experiences that move beyond the transactional to the truly unforgettable. A must-read for everyone involved in events. Especially for those interested in hearing great stories!

Dr Catriona Campbell MBE,
Partner, EY

SASHA FRIEZE

THE CHIEF EVENT OFFICER'S PLAYBOOK

HOW TO CREATE
TRANSFORMATIONAL EVENTS

First published in Great Britain by Practical Inspiration Publishing, 2026

© Sasha Frieze, 2026

The moral rights of the author have been asserted.

9781788606912 (paperback)
9781788606905 (hardback)
9781788606936 (ebook)

All rights reserved. This book, or any portion thereof, may not be reproduced without the express written permission of the publisher.

Every effort has been made to trace copyright holders and to obtain their permission for the use of copyright material. The publisher apologizes for any errors or omissions and would be grateful if notified of any corrections that should be incorporated in future reprints or editions of this book.

EU GPSR representative: LOGOS EUROPE, 9 rue Nicolas Poussin, LA ROCHELLE 17000, France Contact@logoseurope.eu

Want to bulk-buy copies of this book for your team and colleagues? We can customize the content and co-brand *The Chief Event Officer's Playbook* to suit your business's needs.

Please email info@practicalinspiration.com for more details.

For Darren and Josh

Contents

About the author   xvii

Preface   xix

Introduction: Why do Chief Event Officers matter?   1

Part 1: Why are you creating this event?   21

Chapter 1. Exploring the event transformation   23

Chapter 2. Envisioning the journey   41

Chapter 3. Articulating the purpose   59

Part 2: Who is the event for?   81

Chapter 4. Mapping the stakeholders   83

Chapter 5. Amplifying the message   103

Part 3: What will the event experience be?   131

Chapter 6. Curating the content   133

Chapter 7. Crafting the experience   161

Chapter 8. Reimagining the welcome   183

Part 4: How do you build impact beyond the event? 199

Chapter 9. Evaluating your transformational outcome 201

Chapter 10. Making events a board-level conversation 215

Acknowledgements 223

Notes 225

Bibliography 233

Index 235

Event Transformation Blueprint

About the author

Sasha Frieze FRSA FCIM is an award-winning event strategist, delivering 1,000+ events in 30+ years. Sasha has worked for decades with clients across media owners, corporates, associations and non-profits. Her clients include the United Nations Foundation, *The Guardian*, *The BMJ*, the Open Data Institute, Aberdeen Investments, Raymond James, Incisive Media, Informa, the British Society for Immunology and the Royal College of Anaesthetists.

Sasha is a Non-Executive Director of the British Society for Haematology, a Fellow of both the Chartered Institute of Marketing and The Royal Society of Arts, a visiting lecturer in event management at The University of Westminster, London, and a frequent speaker at industry events.

Sasha runs The Business Narrative, a consulting firm for organizations looking for strategies and ideas to create transformational events.

Preface

What is an event?

Your best friend's wedding. 135,000 people at Comicon. My dad's 50-year college reunion. 650 insurance and allied professionals at ILC's Specialist Subsidence Conference.

Anywhere people connect, convene, share an experience.

From Glastonbury Festival and celebrity weddings to the European Society of Cardiology Congress – the world's biggest gathering of heart specialists – and Allen & Company's Sun Valley Conference. From La Tomatina tomato festival in Buñol near Valencia to the British Queen's Platinum Jubilee celebration in 2022. And everything in between.

The events industry is fragmented, valued at over $1.2 trillion in 2024, employing millions of people globally and constantly developing.[1]

The focus of this book is on business and professional events, typically those with content at the heart of them. What used to be called B2B (business to business), although the world has evolved and such divisions are neither clearcut nor helpful.

The word 'conference' puts me in mind of an ornately decorated windowless ballroom in the nineties with over-brewed tea and packet biscuits served at the back of the room. Of speakers tapping the mic and plaintively asking 'is this thing working?' Of overstuffed agendas, queues for the bathroom and warm wine at the mandatory VIP drinks. Where everyone is a VIP. And everyone drinks.

Words are laden with meaning. Exhibitions, tradeshows and fairs speak of unrecyclable brightly coloured one-use carpet and salespeople who are either too in-your-face or too shy to be on the show floor. Hiding. Of sometimes hard-sell 'solution-led' presentations.

Summits, symposia, fora; more academic, clinical or civil society events with dense programmes of occasionally dry content and not enough time to breathe.

In recent years, we've developed new language around gatherings and experiences. Gentler words for our more creative and nuanced times.

I'll use all these words interchangeably. I invite you to let go of any pre-conceptions you may have about events and their predetermined models. I invite you to think afresh and journey with me as we explore how to create impactful events that help change the world.

Another note on the word 'attendee'. Joe Pine[2] reminded me that a participant takes an active part in a gathering. The events industry is very attached to the words 'delegate' and 'attendee'. Delegates are quite old school; attendee implies presence but not necessarily engagement. I'll use all three words in this book and invite you to lean towards participants.

****

This book is about event strategy. How getting clarity on your event's desired transformation, journey and purpose can help you craft impactful gatherings – creating a chain of events that ultimately lead to genuine change.

This is not a book about event logistics, operations or budgeting. You won't find guidance on negotiating venue contracts or subvention in a new city, how many croissants to order or how to write a request for proposal for audio visual at a 3,000 person event. There's no event tech guide or data management plan.

These things are incredibly important. They are part of the vast suite of skills event strategists/planners/producers/directors and, of course, Chief Event Officers may have and need. I value my logistics and operations colleagues and the enormous skills they bring to the team.

But if you want your events to deliver on your bold ambition – and I will argue that events without a clarity of purpose are unlikely be successful anyway – then this book is designed to take you through 10 core principles that will help you think about how to create exceptional events that deliver an intentional impact.

To help you apply these ten core principles I've created the Event Transformation Blueprint, featuring 13 frameworks. Wherever you see this icon ⬇, visit https://chiefeventofficer.co/resources to access the corresponding template or worksheet or scan the QR code below. Use them with your team to drive your event's transformation.

Introduction: Why do Chief Event Officers matter?

Emergence of the Chief Event Officer

The emergence of the Chief Event Officer signals the arrival of a new board-level conversation – how will we best use our events to help us deliver on our bigger purpose?

There's a change happening in the world of events, gatherings and experiences.

A growing understanding that says – excellent operational event delivery is a given; what counts is creating gatherings and experiences that help create transformational change. It's time to have a bigger strategic conversation at every level of the organization exploring how events, experiences and activations can be intentionally designed to create meaningful outcomes.

Gatherings are increasingly perceived as the most important marketing tool for organizations – delivering both strategic outcomes and community.

According to research, 78% of event professionals consider in-person events the most impactful marketing channel, 80% say they're a critical component of their organization's success, and 83%

report that in-person B2B conferences, summits and conventions are the most effective way to build and grow community.[1]

In the age of automation and AI perhaps we're all looking for events that elevate our human connection. We're all searching for belonging, community and meaning.

If you are the Chief Marketing Officer (CMO) or other board member or senior leader, I invite you to explore the difference gatherings can make to delivering your strategic objectives.

If you have responsibility for your gathering's strategy or your event business' strategy (or you aspire to) step into the Chief Event Officer mindset and sit with the CMO, CEO and senior executives, talking the language of business and the difference events can make.

The Chief Event Officer's Playbook is a guide to help you harness your curiosity, thinking, creativity and purpose.

I invite you to follow this blueprint to ensure that your event becomes part of a bigger conversation around event strategy for your organization – how your gatherings can help deliver your bigger purpose.

Events are where the trust is

Beyond AI and misinformation

We live in an age of deep fakes. Misinformation. Live events are where real people have authentic conversations. Where the trust is.[2]

Information overwhelm

The world has changed since we sought fascinating facts in the library.

Today's issue isn't *finding* the information; it's evaluating, assessing, *curating* that information.

But where do you start? And how long will it take? Of course, you can write an AI prompt to sift for you, but how will you know if it's accurate?

And there's a time/money trade off. Professional life is busier and more demanding. While you might theoretically be open to writing a great AI prompt and taking a view on the content outputs, wouldn't you rather a group of smart people did the work for you? And added nuance to that information – so events are not just presentations, they're a convening of the leaders in your field debating issues live.

The complexity of every field, and the volume of data, issues and people can be overwhelming. TMI (too much information). Infobesity. Infoxication. Information anxiety.

A friend in a niche area of professional services – one where there used to be one journal, and if you'd read it, you were up-to-date – told me recently that it's now almost impossible to keep up with the journals, digital journals, blogs, websites, Substacks, Medium/ Media and WhatsApp group links.

One of the big drivers of content-led events is that, done well, that content has been researched and curated for you. And the best events have teams of curious smart, well-connected and thoughtful content producers.

Simplifying the complex and bringing the right speakers and facilitators to explore those conversations is a major factor in attending events.

How many times have you read the words 'in just one day out of the office, you can learn...'?

In our complex times simplicity is intoxicating.

Seeking authenticity

Events' authenticity trumps every other channel.

The attendee experience has changed in the last few decades. Thirty years ago, delegates were (largely) men-in-suits, and we treated them basically as their job title, rather than individuals.

Different times. Participants are people, consumers, individuals first. And while Boomers and Gen X-ers may have a more traditional approach, there are new kids on the block. There's a generational shift among event attendees.

Events, and how people engage with them, have been on a journey. Since the boom of business events in the last decades there's been a marked change in the event participant experience. Here's my 'Event Evolution Model.'

The Event Evolution Model

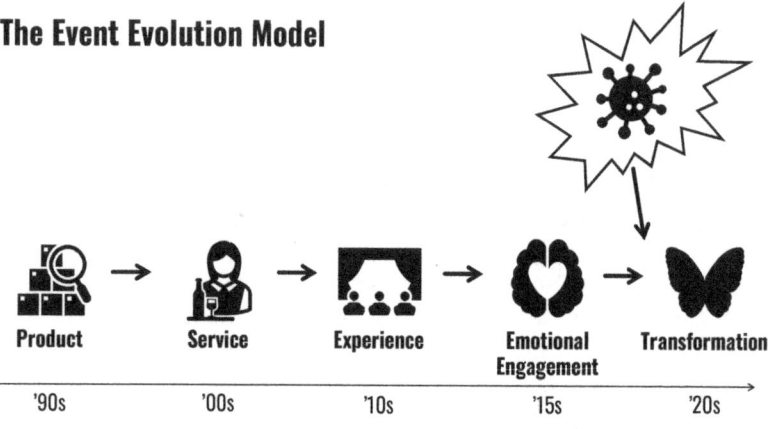

Product	Service	Experience	Emotional Engagement	Transformation
'90s	'00s	'10s	'15s	'20s

Millennials and Gen Z are 'next gen event goers' (NGEG) according to the Freeman Trends Report;[3] they will form 75% of the workforce by 2030.

We need to design events that understand NGEGs and their desires – which I think we all have, deep down – for personal connection, impact and purpose, authenticity.

Compared to other channels – marketing, advertising, social – events are real. They can't be AI'd.

In our tech-led world, in-person events are the last bastion of real, personal, connection.

In-person events create trust. Relationships. Authenticity.

The recent EY report on Gen Z highlighted how authenticity is Gen Z's most important value.[4] And that extends beyond the

- ▶ 1980s–1990s – **Events as a product**: events were undifferentiated, transactional and commodified, based on pre-internet knowledge exchange or connections. Largely homogenous and the delegates were, too.

- ▶ 1990s–2000s – **Events as a service**: Differentiation through customer service and delegate/speaker/ partner relationships.

- ▶ 2010s – **Events as an experience**: The lightbulb moment; events weren't just about the content, but how they made people feel. A new focus on the entire event lifecycle, injecting experience-driven touchpoints.

- ▶ 2015 onwards – **Events as emotional engagement**: No more soulless corporate talk. The best events now resonated with the *person*, not just the job title, sparking genuine emotional connections. Designing events that made people feel something

- ▶ 2022 onwards – **Events as a transformation**: Post-pandemic, participants want return on investment (ROI) on their time and attention. The best events don't just inform – they *shift* perspectives, promising game-changing impact. If it's not transformational, why bother?

individuals themselves; they want everyone to be empowered to be their authentic selves.

And they want authentic experiences. For authentic experiences, read live events. Live events are the ultimate expression of authenticity. There's no hiding behind AI or digital.

And that's why corporates and non-profits are betting the farm on in-person events right now. They're the only channel where all the noise is stripped away. Leaving the signal, the in-person connection, conversation, community.

That's where the magic happens.

How I learned about community

I grew up in a small, vibrant community in the north of England. I always knew I was part of something.

We knew our neighbours – I called them and my parents' friends auntie and uncle. When I got home from school my mum was usually next door, or Auntie Deanne was having a cup of tea round our kitchen table. My school years were basically one very long cup of tea. Hospitality and connection were baked into my childhood experience. Also, baking. For a long time I thought there was a fourth meal in the day – tea – drinks, biscuits, sandwiches. And lots and lots of conversation.

My parents – and grandparents – contributed to our community; my mum took older people to hospital appointments, organized meals for those in need and did errands for sick people. She and Auntie Ida were total powerhouses. Well before the events industry was a thing they could organize anything – a communal meal for 200? No problem. Also, no computers, it was all in their heads – Auntie Ida used to write out a 'fair copy' of the notes at the end of the meeting.

My dad volunteered for many local community organizations, was a governor of more than one school and spent most of his evenings in meetings with local VIPs, helping change things for the better.

My parents' combined message to us was this: community counts. It's a relationship – it goes both ways. You don't always get back exactly what you put in, but it doesn't matter. Have no expectations – make your contribution because it's the right thing to do.

Also, treat everyone with kindness. It doesn't matter if someone is the CEO or the cleaner, everybody's input counts. This is where I learned about high-performing teams and playing to people's strengths.

When you have a pot-luck communal meal and that nice woman who really can't cook brings a very unappealing quiche, don't let her leave feeling bad. Quietly take a slice or two out of the quiche so she can go home feeling good about herself and her cooking.

These are the values I took with me into the world of events. Community. Connection. Meaning. Hospitality. Respect and kindness. They have served me well.

Gatherings are communities

My first real job was as a marketing manager for IIR, an Informa precursor, crafting marketing plans for ultra-niche financial and professional events – communities. I learned that each event was its own small world. Each had its own newsletters and publications, micro-communities, influencer-types, leaders and followers.

I found it easy to connect with speakers and editors because they all cared about their communities too. We spoke the same language. I built relationships.

I researched the niche-iest niche publication, that delivered phenomenal ROI, off the back of a suggestion from a leader in the environmental regulation field (I still remember her name). (I also spent a very long time looking for a magazine a conference producer recommended to me called *Broadcast News* (which is a film) because the internet had not yet been invented.)

I learned how to forensically analyse markets, how to listen to delegates and how to write long copy (which converts better than short copy, still).

But what I really learned, many years later, reflecting on the arc of my career is that it wasn't by accident that I was drawn to the world of B2B pureplay conferences.

What I was drawn to was community.

Every event and gathering had its own ecosystem, tribes and networks. I learned that it is a privilege to be invited into those worlds, and to see them from the inside, not as a supplier.

That insight – that gatherings are communities – has travelled with me throughout my career, helping me serve employers and clients.

Never forget that it is an honour to be invited into the worlds you create and serve those communities as they journey to make change in their professional lives.

Putting events at the core of your organization

It's no secret to media owners that the print ad revenue model is broken. The 2023 WARC report showcases that print ad revenue has halved in the six years to 2023.[5] While there has been a vast reduction in such revenue, there has only been a modest increase in digital ad revenues for the growing online 'oligopoly' of tech giants and retailers (Amazon, Alphabet, Meta).

With fewer print ads and only a modest increase in digital ads, response rates to digital channels are declining. CMOs are turning their attention to channels that can deliver – increasingly seeing events as a crucial tool in the comms arsenal. A channel that can deliver measurable change and outcomes.

Commercial conference and trade show organizations have live events at the heart of their business model. In fact, commercializing the relationships at events *is* the business model. However, even with decades of expertise, they are seeing that to engage attendees' attention they need to develop their value offering to ensure relevance.

Associations and non-profits also view convening their members as a core activity. However, they are increasingly facing competition from media owners and commercial event companies, or even their own corporate partners hosting their own events.[6]

Lines are blurred. Business models are changing. And it seems that the power of in-person is attractive, yet also competitive. Positioned well, events are highly lucrative – for commercial organizers, for corporates developing business, for associations growing their membership.

Whether you are an event specialist at a corporate, media owner, commercial conference or trade show organization or an association or non-profit, the time has come to elevate the conversation and put events at the core of your organization's strategy.

Are business and professional events broken?

Worlds change. Markets mature. Technology simplifies and automates. As sectors evolve and businesses make acquisitions and standardize, corporatization can lead to things feeling samey.

If you build it they won't necessarily come.

Participants won't automatically attend your conference or exhibition because they came last year. The 63rd edition of your Annual Congress is not a good enough reason to entice people to plan a trip and be out of the office for a week.

Participants crave a whole host of different motivators for attendance: something that speaks to them both individually and professionally, a deep desire for connection and a sense of community, curated insight that you can't get trawling online and the ever present something 'new'.

The pandemic was a circuit breaker in the world of events.

E3, the once-mighty Electronic Entertainment Expo, was the heartbeat of the gaming world, pulling in 70,000 attendees at its peak. LA's annual gaming extravaganza was where publishers, developers and hardware giants pulled back the curtain on their biggest reveals – think Keanu Reeves announcing his Cyberpunk 2077 role in 2019 or Mario creator Shigeru Miyamoto bringing Ubisoft's Davide Soliani to tears in 2017.

Cracks appeared in the early 2000s when exhibitors grumbled about the lack of actual retailers and journalists, leading to a disastrous 2006 downsizing. The show bounced back, but the cost of flashy booths sent big players running to host their own events (looking at you, EA Play). Sony bailed in 2019, and Covid dealt the final blow. By December 2023, E3 was officially dead – struggling to stay relevant in an industry that had outgrown it. Like Comdex before it, it fell victim to high costs, shifting trends and a failure to innovate. Game over.[7]

A lesson to today's Chief Event Officers to keep their eye on the bigger strategic objectives – the purpose and vision – and to listen to your audiences. Stay curious. Keep innovating.

I've spent years asking people in the events world one question: tell me about a transformational event you've hosted or attended.

The answers? Electric. The energy is instant, the excitement tangible. Even if the event happened decades ago, the memory still fizzes with enthusiasm.

Take British businessman Piers Linney. He raves about the Microsoft Worldwide Partner Conference, where his business snagged Global Hosting Partner of the Year in 2010.

'My mind was blown', he recalls, dazzled by the scale, the movers and shakers, the sheer potential.[8] But time marches on. The event morphed into Microsoft Inspire, first as a digital-only affair, then rebranded and fused with Microsoft Ignite in 2024 for a hybrid experience. There's now MCAPS Start for Partners, a fresh digital venture.

Yet when Piers talks about Anthropy, his excitement rockets to another level. 'It's not a business event,' he insists (though, let's be honest, it is – just not in the usual stale format). Instead, it's about people, prosperity, planet and purpose. 'Number one is the location. It's in Cornwall, not Excel at lunchtime. Once you're there, it's a commitment. Dinner in the biomes at the Eden Project is amazing.'

Anthropy, launched by John O'Brien to drive post-pandemic renewal, now draws 2,000+ attendees and has evolved into a national network. It's not a cookie-cutter gathering – it's a creatively conceived community experience with transformation, stories and purpose at its heart. What every business event *should* be.

Throughout these pages we'll take inspiration from a huge range of events, hosted by a broad variety of organizations, each with their own agenda. Size doesn't matter; we can learn from anyone. Indeed, intimate and exclusive micro events (fewer than 50 participants) are sometimes where the best business and connections happen.

And we'll be seeking out those gatherings that can inspire us to innovate, to design events that create the moment to change perspectives.

What's driving these changes?

Tech development has had an enormous impact on the events industry – the event tech stack includes everything from registration, ticketing, speaker and content management, data management and analysis, marketing and Customer Relationship Management (CRM) systems, calls for papers, networking, matching and engagement to on-site check-ins and post-event analysis.

Technology has both reduced barriers to entry for new market entrants and created automations that can reduce human involvement, ultimately leading to a samey-ness for some events. Also, when the tech works, it's great. When the integration breaks? Frustrating. The pandemic-enabled speedy rise of dozens of online event platforms (hello, Hopin) helped event planners to deliver digital events. Hallelujah.[9]

Event planners are among the most innovative professions – how a global industry 'pivoted' to deliver community and connection in the face of a once-in-a-century pandemic is a Netflix series waiting to happen.

But online fatigue set in. Attendees didn't want 'Zoom and crisps' anymore; they wanted an engaging, immersive experience. Many event producers harnessed the skills of advertising and film professionals, branded broadcast studios and TV production skills.

In fact, there's data to support my supposition that online experiences are less meaningful.

Neuroscientist Paul Zak, an expert in measurement, told me, 'We did the work pre-Covid; online gives you 50–80% of the experience compared to in-person.'[10] In fact, virtual events are now often designed to supplement the in-person experience.

And that left us with the spectre of hybrid events – attempting to be all things to all people and meaning something different to everyone. TLDR (too long; didn't read); I believe you need to decide which audience to privilege – online or in-person – and design the event from there.[11]

One pleasing result of the pandemic is the 'new normal' of recording nearly all the content, broadcasting key sessions to an online audience and creating content that gives marketing teams untold gold.

Of course, the world was already fractured before Covid.

Extreme weather, combined with the climate crisis, has an impact on both travel and sustainability decisions. Let's face it, sustainability (or the lack of it) has been the dirty secret of event production for many years, until recently.

The tectonic plates of geopolitical shifts have an impact. Global conflicts and diplomatic pressures have a significant impact on business as it's increasingly globalized. The Russo–Ukraine war, the Israel–Gaza war, Syria, the humanitarian crisis in Yemen, civil war in Sudan.

These all impact economic stability, the global supply chain, business confidence and travel.

There are generational differences in both approach to employment and personal style in relation to work. There is a growing commitment to diversity, equity and inclusion; greater awareness of neurodiversity and different personality types.

Ever shortening attention spans.

Societal polarization. Talk of culture wars. In the UK, Brexit. Trade wars and tariffs.

All of these drivers require events to respond. What participants and event partners want is changing, and Chief Event Officers need to keep their finger on the pulse.

Purpose as a commercial driver has come of age

Philosophers explore the human desire to do something purposeful as an innate need to search for meaning in life.[12]

Since the 1980s, the principles of corporate social responsibility (CSR) and environmental, social and governance (ESG) have gained traction in the corporate world. CSR was coined in the 1950s,[13] and the concept of ESG was first used in the early 2000s.[14]

Businesses now automatically report on CSR and ESG, with sustainability reports integrated in their annual financial reports, including environmental impact and social initiatives, using established frameworks like the GRI[15] or SASB.[16]

This broader approach, combined with the arrival of the Chief Purpose Officer and Chief Vision Officer in many large organizations, heralds the arrival of a gentler world, one where sustainability, meaning and purpose are the language of many organizations.

Or as author Joe Pine says, 'the future of business is transforming lives, not selling stuff.'[17]

Business events are about being ahead of trends. And in a world where (client) organizations and individuals are changing, event strategists and their teams are changing too, often ahead of the curve.

Businesses and organizations are taking operational excellence for granted – led by the Chief Operating Officer (COO) and the Chief Financial Officer (CFO) – and moving their focus towards meaning and purpose, employing Chief Vision Officers and Chief Purpose Officers to drive the agenda.

And so now is the time for event owners to ensure that their event strategies focus on delivering the bigger purpose.

The 5Cs of a meaningful journey

The 'gatherings are communities' philosophy has helped me create a model to help us understand what makes an event truly transformational, a model for any future Chief Event Officer to use. For the business or professional event journey to be impactful, I believe five core event elements are ideally required.

The 5Cs of a transformational event

▶ **Content** – is the magic sauce of your gathering. Whether that's presentations or fireside chats or intentionally designing ways for people to connect, it's a big chunk of what draws people to attend.

▶ **Connection** – the ability to meet other people in person and your ability to enable that is what brings participants to your event. Whether it's networking, dinners, the app or the myriad other ways you do it, it's vital.
If your event *only* offers content and connection then it's basically a webinar. If I can watch a presentation and chat in the chat – why would I leave the house? If it should be a webinar, let it be a webinar.

▶ **Celebration** – today's authentic participants, speakers and partners are looking for events that feel celebratory, personal and entertaining. Whether that's the Royal Welcome[18] at the World Experience Summit – noble ladies from Queen Marie Antoinette's court greet you with tossed lavender, rose-scented mist and violet candy to prepare you for your audience at court – or your ability to get a massage after a busy day of sessions, an event designed to meet you personally not just professionally. Also, good for socials.
So the award-winning agency CEO at Cannes Lions Festival holding up the WhatsApp-branded ice cream is Instagram magic.

▶ **Community** – The power of belonging is huge. Association gatherings thrive on inbuilt community, while corporate events craft them by targeting the right people. Media-owned and commercial events? The best ones are doing this brilliantly. But for some, it's marketing over meaning.

▶ **Ceremony** – Some events are unmissable, the ones everyone marks in their calendar. They nail the 5Cs – especially ceremony, celebrating industry stars through awards; 'Thirty Under Thirty' lists or exclusive gatherings. It's prestige, recognition and a little necessary ego boost.

A true Hot Ticket event blends all five elements, creating an experience that's authentic, fulfilling and impossible to skip.

Future Proof Festival is a great example of a '5C' gathering. Launched in 2021, it's billed as the world's largest gathering of wealth management professionals.[19] It's a four-day festival – the industry's only outdoor event, literally on the beach – that brings together financial advisors and limited partners (LPs). The Coachella of wealth events.

Future Proof delivers innovative content – 80% C-level speakers sharing real insights, no 'pay for play' – and great connection through facilitating over 37,000 1:1 Breakthru Meetings, with a 95% meeting satisfaction rate.

The festival atmosphere in Huntingdon Beach, California, creates a party vibe. One delegate said, 'I've never been part of a conference where I felt a greater sense of community.' Another called it 'Disney World for independent minded Advisors. An amazing place.'

As the welcome copy says: 'every moment at Future Proof is built to maximize your impact and growth.'

And the Festival is part of the Future Proof family which pioneers unique formats including city-wide events and curated retreats. All designed to deliver transformational experiences for the wealth management eco-system.

Curated learning

The *Playbook* aims to bring together learnings from across the five core categories of business events, as well as stories of consumer experiences that can help inspire Chief Event Officers.

The range of event-hosting organizations is ever-expanding. Clarifying and articulating your transformation has different complexities depending on the nature of your organization.

Corporate events: purpose-driven and evolving

Corporate events typically have clear objectives – global partner summits or sales conferences. They fall into three categories:

- ▶ Third-party events – sponsorships, speaking, exhibiting
- ▶ Hosted customer events – user groups, client conferences
- ▶ Internal events – offsites, parties, team-building, all-hands meetings

With remote work rising, internal events are booming.[20]

And everything in-between; there are corporate events that sell tickets to participants and sponsorships to partners in their supply chain, taking more of a commercial approach.

Associations and non-profits: built for change

Transformation is often hardwired into these organizations; making it compelling requires finesse. A vague 'changing the air conditioning supply sector' won't excite attendees. The key? Collaborate with policy and research teams to craft thoughtful, inspiring events – especially in competitive industries.[21]

Media-owned events: profit meets prestige

With ad revenue dwindling, media companies are investing in branded events as profit drivers. Traditional advertiser-led events have been leveraged into partner event teams, while others have built standalone event businesses, using their editorial prowess and brand authority to attract both speakers and audiences.

Trade shows and conferences: the business of connection

Commercial conferences thrive by knowing their market and audience and convening them to do business. Driven by a commercial imperative, they have a range of subsidiary business models and huge array of approaches to doing this.

Government and policy events: driving impact

Government events often set agendas and shape policy. The UK's 2023 AI Safety Summit tackled AI risks, while the Queen's Platinum Jubilee Pageant in 2022 celebrated societal shifts. These events aren't just gatherings – they aim to leave a lasting mark.

The Chief Event Officer mindset

Events cut across every business and organization. Executed flawlessly, they bring organizations, communities and sectors to life, and so event strategists need to work right across the business to bring every team to play its part.

And it's precisely *because* gatherings are so all-encompassing that where they sit in an organization, and the job titles of the people who deliver them, differ so broadly.

ICE – the In House Corporate Events awards and network – asked 120 event leaders what their job title was. They got 92 different job titles back – all for the exact same role and remit.

So whether you're an event manager or an event marketing manager. An event director, an event planner or an event strategist. Whether you work in an event function, or a marketing function, a strategy function, or an operations function.

Whether you're a Chief Marketing Officer or a Chief Vision Officer. A Chief Strategy Officer or a Chief Operating Officer. A Chief Executive Officer, or a member of the board, the senior leadership team, or a senior executive in a large organization.

If you're reading this, then you're interested in asking the question 'How do I help my teams and organizations shape gatherings that are aligned with our overarching vision?'

Get the strategy right

When business, association and event professionals align the event objectives with the organizational objectives, they design gatherings where the magic happens – the energy, the conversations, the business deals, the relationships. The excitement.

Money follows strategy. When I see events fail, it's typically through lack of clarity. If you don't know what you're trying to achieve, your participants, sponsors and partners won't want to get involved.

But when you have total, laser focus on your event's big purpose, you've heard your audience's needs and you deliver that phenomenal event – there are many examples in this book – then, typically, it's profitable (or surplus creating).

Introducing the *Playbook*

The Chief Event Officer's Playbook is a tool to help drive your strategic process, asking four questions to help shape your event design.

- ▶ Why are you creating this event?

- ▶ Who is the event for?

- ▶ What is the event experience?

- ▶ How do you build impact beyond the event?

Each question has subsidiary questions, and these 10 pillars are here to guide you, as a Chief Event Officer, senior leader or C-suite executive as you create transformational gatherings that deliver your big vision.

Stepping into your gatherings' strategic power

It's time to think of events differently. No longer a cost centre, but a purpose centre.

Just as marketing is a company-wide function – typically sitting within the framework of corporate strategy and translating an organization's overall vision into strategies and plans that reach and engage customers and drive impact and outcomes – the same is true for events.

It's time to increase the strategic rigour we bring to our gatherings; we take excellent event execution as a given.

Our events' successes hinge on these four questions that underpin their strategic success.

Let's dive in.

PART 1
WHY ARE YOU CREATING THIS EVENT?

Chapter 1
Exploring the event transformation

Events. Gatherings. Conferences. Experiences. Exhibitions. Fairs. Summits. Trade Shows. Symposia. Offsites. Internal meetings. Whatever the nature of your business or non-profit event, for it to have a big impact or a lasting legacy it needs to change something.

For your event to step into its power and be more than 'venue and menu' or 'chalk and talk', it needs to have clarity on the transformation it makes. And you'll want to invest in determining what that is.

Three questions, one strategy

Starting with a blank piece of paper can seem overwhelming. You've got a jumble of ideas. You've got a great feeling that those ideas can coalesce into something successful. You know you want to bring people together physically, to create spaces for conversations. To help participants share new approaches. You have a sense that your event can generate genuine impact.

But where do you start?

Why are you creating this event? There are three questions that underpin your strategy process. What is the transformation? What is the journey? What is your event's purpose?

The first step in *The Chief Event Officer's Playbook* is to understand the transformation you want to make. Whether this is for your participants, your organization or your sector, clarifying your transformation and who it's for is the first step in your thousand-mile journey.

And I don't have to tell you, events have a thousand moving parts.

The first three cogs in the wheel – transformation, journey and purpose – form the core questions that drive your strategy.

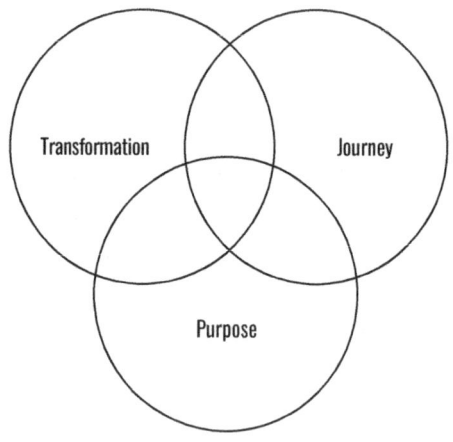

How transformation, journey and purpose relate

Are you bought into needing a purpose?

Your event needs a purpose, a vision. Something that gets it out of bed in the morning.

Bernardo Mariano Joaquim Junior is United Nations (UN) Chief Information Technology Officer and perfectly placed to see a need: to encourage collaboration in the open source community, especially around what he calls 'Neglected Open Source tools' – used for critical digital public infrastructure but often without the robust organizations behind them which minimize risk. Bernardo told me,[1] 'We never talk about neglected resources – until there's a cyber security incident.'

The OSPOs for Good Summit 2023 initiative was born in partnership with OSPO++ and Open Forum Europe. Connecting Open Source Program Offices globally with diverse open source thinkers, policymakers, government agencies and tech companies. The aim: to leverage open source technology for positive societal impact, all in service of the UN's Sustainable Development Goals (SDGs).

The UN harnessed its convening power to advance OSPOs for Good, evolving into UN Open Source Week 2024. They began identifying unsupported critical open-source tools, while a hackathon engaged young people in using open-source solutions to tackle global challenges. Bernardo shaped an event that delivered a vision.

In the events sector's infancy, people were just excited to meet.

In 1991, I ran a team that created hundreds of legal conferences each year. We organized the IBC Legal Studies Employment Law Update, and there were over 500 people in the largest room at London's Café Royale (now a luxury hotel and private members club, then a series of faded meeting rooms that smelled slightly of school dinners). Delegates waited with bated breath for *the* event – the annual update was the only place you could get all the latest legal changes, their implications, checklists and conversations with peers who cared as much as you.

Participants loved the knowledge, the Continuing Professional Development (CPD) points and the networking. They loved the sit-down lunch – usually chicken in a white wine sauce. We did not know many vegetarians.

Nowadays, that's a webinar.

The pace of change in the last three decades has been enormous. Think back to the Event Evolution Model – today's events need to do more than share information; more than just convene people, even over a swanky lunch.

An event that connects with people and inspires them to go away and do something needs to have a deliberate transformation. We need to be intentional in articulating the purpose, journey and desired transformation, and then – and only then – designing the format, the flow and the mechanics of the event, to deliver a specific outcome.

What is the headline transformation you'd like to see?

Grab a notebook or a phone app and start braindumping: what is the big transformation? What are you aiming to change? What does your event *do*?

Hang on to these notes – it will be useful further along the process to compare your initial ideas with where your thinking arrives after exploring the *Playbook* steps: the transformation, all elements of the journey and the purpose.

The scale of your event is not important; what counts is the change you envision.

The Queen's Women's Network was founded in 1979, the year women were first admitted to the College. With 7,000 alumni, engaging them in career guidance has been a challenge. The goal has been to involve more young alumni and women while adding value for current students, broadening opportunities for the future.

Claire Craig, Provost at The Queen's College, Oxford, told me about the 2024 Queen's Women Network Speed Dating, designed to forge transformative connections between students (men as well as women), recent graduates and older alumni.[2] The College had not previously had significant ways of enabling all students to benefit from the experiences of its alumni.

Held in the historic Upper Library, the event was meticulously choreographed – 12 alumni spoke for three minutes each, before moving to individual library booths. Small student groups rotated every five minutes, hearing twelve unique career journeys.

'It was a rapid-fire experience,' Claire said. 'Students saw a range of possible life paths. The conversations that followed sparked new ideas for them.' The event helped redefine alumni–student relationships and expanded the College's role in career support.

Who is the transformation for?

Whatever your gathering's sector, vision or purpose, it seems to me that there are three possibilities when it comes to articulating your transformation and who it's for – three transformation categories.

First, is the transformation for **individuals**, your participants? Does your gathering intentionally make a significant change to people's lives? Learning, meeting, doing business? Is your event about orchestrated serendipity? Or about convening conversations between unusual sparring partners helping generate new ideas? Or is it about inspiring individuals to get involved in a campaign, a movement, a moment?

Second, your **organization**. Are you seeking to transform your organization or association? Are you looking to train 5,000 data analysts in the next three years? Are you looking to grow your event's commercial footprint? Are you seeking to claim or expand market share for your technology, product or service? Are you the meeting place where investors and startups connect? Is your event where deals get made?

Are you the go-to place where corporates and medical researchers connect to explore how to share resources on solving specific issues? This would increase your organization's value in the sector, while also impacting the sector.

As one corporate CMO said to me – 'when I'm bringing together the senior leadership team, how do I make this something that transforms, that moves the organization forward on its journey? Not just a jolly where everyone loves the wine.'

Does your event help participants take their organization from 0 to 60 on the circular economy journey?

Your transformation might be: getting organizations to understand how to positively engage in circular economy practices for both ESG and commercial benefits.

You might pack your event with experts sharing their knowledge, insight and case studies so that participants leave inspired and ready to take action. And you'll create the right frameworks and checklists to help teams hit the ground running. You might even develop a pledge or campaign to amplify the conversation – great for socials and gives you a long tail of content once the event is over.

And finally, the **sector**. Is your event aiming to make policy changes or encourage governmental changes? This is true for many associations and party political events. Does your event seek to resolve systemic sectoral issues as a result of the myriad changes in the global supply chain?

Is it designed to effect change in the industry?

Catherine Mayer, a British-American author, activist and journalist, is a prolific initiator; co-founder and President of the former Women's Equality Party and a co-founder of the Primadonna Festival with Jane Dyball.

In 2019, Catherine and Jane, two of the festival's co-founders, aimed to create a more representative, inclusive and imaginative literary arena for writers and readers of all kinds. It's a platform for creativity, connection and positive change. The festival's mission is to specifically give prominence to groups traditionally disadvantaged in the arts by their background or circumstance. It serves as a catalyst for change in the literary world, promoting inclusivity and providing tangible opportunities for marginalized voices to be heard and celebrated.

Or as Catherine described it to me, 'We set out to be fully and passionately inclusive from the beginning.'[3] And the great tag line (purpose proposition) she crafted was 'the world as it should be for one weekend.'

While your event can have multiple audiences and may be a mix of any or all of the transformation categories – individual, organization and sector – I'd encourage you to have a core focus. Gatherings are most successful when they're not trying to be all things to all people. Let's explore each of these transformational categories in more detail.

Individual transformation

Events change people. Whatever category of participant – delegates, speakers, sponsors and exhibitors, VIPs – the impact can be profound.

How will your participants be transformed? Will they solve an industry problem, gain new insights, or build valuable connections?

Gill Livingston, Professor of Psychiatry of Older People at UCL and a leading dementia researcher, illustrates this beautifully.

Dementia has overtaken cancer as the most feared condition for over-55s in the UK.

Gill told me that what she values most about conferences is the rare opportunity to pause and think.[4] In the whirlwind of academia, clinical work and writing, reflection is a luxury. Conferences, however, create space for deep thought, often sparked by conversations with peers.

At a major psychiatry conference years ago, Gill had time to wrestle with a crucial question: can interventions reduce dementia risk? If so, when in life do they work best? Are early interventions more effective or do later ones still help?

This lightbulb moment was created by a gathering. The coming together of content (speakers, workshops, conversations), community (peers with shared interests) and connection (networking, talking, sharing) created the perfect circumstances. The optimum configuration of people, place, presentations, peers.

That idea, nurtured in a conference hall, led to something remarkable: Gill led the 2017 *Lancet* Commission on Dementia Prevention, followed by Commissions in 2020 and 2024. Her team of 28 global experts have identified 14 modifiable risk factors accounting for 45% of dementias. The report, launched at AAIC 2020, simplified vast research into a compelling infographic and policy recommendations. It's been cited over 16,000 times and influenced government health policy worldwide.

Not every individual will have an insight of this magnitude, but that's not the point. Your goal is to explore the range of transformations your event can spark. Exploring this with your team often leads to powerful event narratives – ones that truly make an impact.

Organizational transformation

Creating a transformative event – for either you as the host organization, or for the businesses attending – can be extraordinarily powerful.

Whether your organizational transformation is about you – more customers, increased membership, a bigger advocacy and policy voice – or for participant organizations, being intentional reaps rewards.

I was approached by a Europe-based scientific association to reimagine their flagship event. Facing competition from global sister societies and commercial rivals, they struggled with declining attendance, weak sponsorship and a lack of clear purpose. Their six-letter acronym held internal meaning but lacked external clarity. Their broad, interdisciplinary sector had no unifying idea.

Organizations can sometimes cling to tradition, losing sight of impact. I led a strategy workshop with their board, mapping competitors, analysing market dynamics and identifying the sector's high monetization potential – explaining the rise in commercial competition. We examined their audiences – delegates, speakers, sponsors, VIPs and the media – and why they were truly gathering.

When asked about purpose, responses were rooted in the past: 'we've always done it this way' or 'we meet in January'. Their website reinforced this inward focus, emphasizing member benefits over broader impact.

We shifted to outward thinking, identifying their unique value: bridging two sectors to drive world-changing science. This insight led to recommendations for a reimagined event – redesigned spaces, new formats fostering interdisciplinary connections and a competition to track resulting collaborations.

The ripple effect was profound. The association refocused on its transformative mission, rebranded with a clear name, adopting their event's big idea as their organizational vision. This alignment helped reinvigorate their standing in the sector.

Transformation begins with identifying and defining an organization's unique value. By simplifying complex messages and aligning strategy with purpose, we turned a struggling event into a platform for innovation and global impact.

It was always there – uncovering and clearly communicating it drives both sector and organizational transformation.

Or sometimes that organizational transformation can have a wider impact, across a geographical region.

Miguel Neves, Editor-in-Chief at Skift Meetings, shared an example of an event he observed that was 'carefully designed with the intention of generating attention and, ultimately, a specific type of investment in the region'.[5]

The International MICE Summit, held in Riadh in December 2024, was designed to attract inward investment into Saudi Arabia and make it a serious player in the global events industry. It was both intentionally transformational and media friendly, with around 20 companies announcing either their intention to host events in Saudi Arabia or to set up local offices.

P&G leverage their annual gathering to encourage continuous improvement, with a creative, disruptive edge.

The annual P&G Signal Summit – welcoming thousands online and in-person at P&G's Cincinnati headquarters – is a catalyst for innovation and strategic growth, shaping the company's future. Curated and hosted by entrepreneur and author John Battelle and P&G Chief Brand Officer Marc Pritchard, its focus is differentiating signal from noise.

Bringing together industry leaders from Walmart, YouTube, the NFL and *The New York Times*, along with internal innovators, the summit fosters continuous improvement and adaptability. It champions creativity and constructive disruption, empowering P&G teams to challenge convention and leverage advanced technologies to enhance operations – ensuring P&G stays at the forefront of consumer goods innovation.

As one online commentator put it, 'I have always been impressed (and pleasantly surprised) by how willing people at P&G are to listen and engage with the new, without ever forgetting their why.'

Sector transformation

Business and professional events have natural sector boundaries.

What 'sector' really means is community – while as individuals we all have different ways of identifying, through our family roles, sports or activities, faith communities, for many of us what we do at work is a big slice of our core identity.

Your participants and partners will likely be heavily invested in your sector community. What are the trends? Although trends can change. What are the drivers? What's changing? Has there been new legislation? A change in government that might affect your world (think education policy). Or a global crisis that brings your sector to the fore (think the world of data pre- and post-pandemic)?

Designing your event to define and create, encourage or support a sector transformation is powerful.

Advertising Week is a series of global events serving the marketing and media – and related technology and culture – communities. Founded in 2004 in New York, its award-winning global event franchise includes Advertising Week New York, Europe and Mexico, plus a series of pop-up versions in other geographies.

Global President Ruth Mortimer talked to me about how Advertising Week was one of the first events to understand that culture drives business and business drives culture, and if you don't get that, you miss out on what's coming next.[6] The show prides itself on interesting content that's a little bit different; Salma Hayek talking about how women are perceived online, Take That talking about how to keep a creative partnership going for 30 years. Nikki Glaser, who was the solo female host of the Golden Globes in January 2025 was doing comedy gigs for Advertising Week in 2019. It's about having their finger on the pulse of culture and how it relates to the world of marketing and media.

Ruth shared how they see the event as creating a transformation in the sector. 'We don't just see ourselves as reflecting the advertising and marketing community, we have a role in making the community that we think should exist. A community that can make more money and do better work.' There are a number of initiatives that are designed to support this; The Future Is Female, free to enter awards, partnerships in the US with Historically Black Colleges and Universities to find the young graduating talent and in the UK, working with Global Purpose Enterprise, unlocking potential for young, diverse people.

Take London Tech Week, a joint venture between Informa Tech[7] and Brent Hoberman's entrepreneur's network, Founders Forum.

London Tech Week – a global gathering of tech and start up execs and their suppliers – opened in June 2023 with Rishi Sunak, then Prime Minster and avowed geek, in conversation with Demis Hassabis, founder of Google DeepMind, AI expert and entrepreneur. A powerful combination.

The show wanted – and got – transformative speakers, to draw the crowds and start the debate at the highest level. They wanted to convene the conversation around tech strategy and AI at the highest level. But Rishi wanted the right stage to talk about his UK Tech Strategy and to set agenda for the AI Safety Summit in November. DeepMind had merged with Google AI's Google Brain division to become Google DeepMind in April of that year, and Demis may have been seeking a platform to demonstrate this transformation. So yes, there's a powerful sector transformation, but underpinned by individual and organizational objectives.

Trends come and go in every sector, and being the person or organization leading those conversations positions you as a leader.

A corporate example: the trend for 'in-housing' advertising, creative and media services. The agency relationship is well understood – clients have objectives, briefs and budgets. Hopefully huge.

Agencies have expertise, experience and staff. Agencies traditionally had lucrative relationships with big brands. And overflowing creative brains. Think TV's *Mad Men*, set in 1960s ad agency land and the client/agency power struggles.

As marketing became more complex, with programmatic, search and social, analytics, data, the thinking began to change. Some big brand CMOs started exploring in-housing. Foregoing or reducing those agency relationships while bringing the marketing, advertising and comms functions in-house.

Conferences sprung up exploring the possibilities. Case studies from who'd had success, what their model was, how it worked. Haymarket's *Campaign* magazine still runs an annual In-Housing Summit as part of its advertising event portfolio.

I was approached to write an event strategy for a major global ad agency. They were looking to create their own agency in-housing gathering; the discussion started in their biz dev (business development) team. The purpose: to change the conversation and ultimately to bring clients into their pipeline.

They were looking to shift the narrative in the CMO world. If Big Agency is inviting Big Brand to a Congress on in-housing, we should all be thinking about it, right?

A meaningful transformation is often predicated on a problem that's seeking a solution.

Here's a challenge that needed a transformation: according to Tech Nation, only 19% of tech workers are women. While 18% of UK IT specialists come from ethnic minority backgrounds, just 11% make it to IT director level.[8] And although 20% of the UK workforce has a disability, only 10% of IT specialists do.

In 2017, Debbie Forster MBE launched the Tech Talent Charter (TTC) to fix what was broken in tech: driving diversity and inclusion in the sector. By April 2024, 822 organizations had signed up. The TTC was industry-led, government-backed and laser-focused on action – arming members with events, resources and real-world strategies.

It wasn't just lip service. TTC's powerhouse partners included the UK government, media heavyweights and top firms across tech, finance and consulting. Its National Event was a bustling in-person hub; post-pandemic, the Inclusion in Tech Festival drew over 1,000 online with meaningful practical takeaways.

The result? A movement. A network. A credible, convening force for change.

However in 2024, the Tech Talent Charter closed, to protest performative diversity, equity and inclusion, urging a sector-wide reset amid widespread organizational 'quiet-quitting' diversity and inclusion strategies due to economic, political and social pressures. The TTC hoped this would serve as a catalyst for renewed commitment to tech sector D&I; the closure itself was a transformational agenda.

Being responsive to changing trends is tough but powerful, and event strategists would be wise to watch their markets and sectors closely. Be ahead of the change, not behind it.

Is your sector transformation a movement?

Events are catalysts that spark ideas, inviting participants to think about issues anew.

If your gathering has a big ambitious idea or a higher aim, that may be something greater than your event.

So the Tech Talent Charter was a movement – an organization leveraging events to create equity for tech employees. It had a position it was advocating, and that gave the events a clarity of purpose. The branding included selfie-frames with the campaign hashtag.

In sectors where people are driving change – GovTech, OSPOs for Good – the language of movements is a great catalyser. And in a world where we all increasingly seek meaning at work, this approach will resonate with many.

If your gathering is genuinely designed to deliver an advocacy aim or create a movement, then say so. But if it's not, don't retrofit. The audience can tell. It's all about being authentic.

What are the big transformation questions?

Your starting point is to explore three overarching questions:

- ▶ What is the big change or transformation you want to achieve?

- ▶ What is the transformative change for individual attendees, your organization or the sector?

- ▶ What's your initial thinking on how you will evaluate whether this transformation was achieved?

⬇ You can explore your event's transformation categories in my **Transformation Category Grid**.

Developing the strategy for your transformative event is like being a sculptor. You start with an enormous piece of rough-hewn marble. Inside, waiting to be discovered, is your perfectly formed gathering. The process of *The Chief Event Officer's Playbook* is to gradually uncover your great work of art.

At this initial stage you're likely talking to varied stakeholders, getting buy-in at different levels of the market. There may be people telling you about a great destination or venue they went to which would be perfect. Nod appreciatively – you already know that you're not going to get to the operational decisions until there's clarity on the event's mission: its transformation, the journey and the stories you'll tell, the competitor context for your event and how it does something different, and how you will articulate all of that into an event narrative or Event Purpose Proposition.

What is your gathering vision?

At this early stage, consider creating your event design with the overall transformation, your big vision, in mind, all with a view to how you might ultimately measure whether you've achieved success.

Artist Max de Esteban, in his work *Extincto*, critiques the assessment and measurement of art's value and its impact on audience engagement. In *7 min*, he highlights how museums use sensors to monitor visitor interaction, determining which artworks remain on display. A piece that holds a viewer's attention for seven minutes receives a top score, influencing exhibition decisions. He argues that quantitative evaluation affects the conception, production and reception of art.

This concept extends beyond museums to events which can also be assessed through data-driven metrics – such as registration patterns, sales leads and session attendance. There is no one-size-fits-all event evaluation criteria. The first response to the questions 'Did your event deliver? Was it a success?' is other questions: what was your event's purpose? What change were you designing your event to make? What was the desired outcome you were seeking?[9]

Stephen Covey's principle, 'begin with the end in mind', reinforces this idea – successful evaluation starts with clearly defined objectives. Chief Event Officers need to think strategically about the transformation, journey and purpose of their event.

⤓ **A Purpose Evaluation Plan** might include various qualitative and quantitative measures to assess the impact and outcomes, ensuring that success is not merely a matter of numbers but of meaningful engagement and change.

This first step is the place to workshop and note your big transformation; what are you trying to achieve? What will your transformed world look like? What changes do you foresee? How do you want your participants to think and feel – and ultimately do different as a result of your event?

Bring the team

Right from the outset, ensure the right people are in the room. Change doesn't happen in isolation – or just from the top. Bring the team.

Too often, event professionals operate in silos – detached from business development in corporates, policy in associations, strategy in commercial media or even sales, marketing and product teams.

Events are a team sport, and *The Playbook* works best with early buy-in. You'll need a mix of voices: your CEO or MD, relevant board members or Non-Executive Directors, and the sharpest minds on your senior leadership team. Who best understands your sector's challenges and opportunities?

Designing transformation should be intentional. If your event has history, you already have a rich source of data – on your audience, your partners, your market. If it's a new concept, your first job is research. What are the key drivers? What big questions need answering? What's keeping your audience awake at night?

Leveraging your transformation thinking

Your focus on understanding the transformation you want to create and who it's for will reap rewards down the line.

You will translate your transformative purpose into your narrative; stories you can tell that are woven into the event marketing and messaging from day one.

Transformation is as much an art as it is a science, and the following chapters will help guide you on frameworks to deliver this and the softer questions and conversations about how to deliver transformational events.

As Abraham Lincoln said, 'Give me six hours to chop down a tree and I will spend the first four sharpening the axe.'

This axe-sharpening will serve you well as you move on from the first step in the *Playbook* to the next questions, helping you develop the journey and ultimately articulate the purpose of your event.

Chapter 2
Envisioning the journey

The second step in *The Chief Event Officer's Playbook* is to envision the participant's journey to support your event strategy's initial phase of thinking.

The participant is at the heart of your event.

The journey step of the *Playbook* considers three core questions:

- ▶ How do you define the journey?

- ▶ How do you articulate that journey through storytelling?

- ▶ How do you ensure that journey is unique by understanding it in the context of its competitors?

A significant driver for creating an event strategy and ultimately an Event Purpose Proposition is to establish and design a gathering that has something new to say to its audience. Every sector is competitive now; it may help to ensure that the gathering you create stands apart from others. Without a clear articulation of your transformation, journey and what's different about your event – what it adds to the universe – your gathering is unlikely to reach its tribe.

This second step helps ensure that your event is the go-to event. Gaining a profound understanding of the participant journey, the story you tell about that journey and putting that journey in context – exploring competitors and establishing how your event is different – will give you the clarity to develop your Event Purpose Proposition at the next stage.

How can you visualize the journey?

With the big transformation in mind the next step is to visualize your participants' journey.

A transformation is by its very nature a journey.

Think of a caterpillar, building a chrysalis and ultimately emerging as a butterfly. That's a true journey of transformation.

Of course there's a starting point and end point. Your participants will be travelling from A to B. More importantly, there's a starting state and ending state. Powerful events that stay with participants change people, change organizations and have an impact. The skill of a Chief Event Officer is to (apparently effortlessly) hard-wire this into the gathering experience.

I think of a Chief Event Officer as somewhere between a master chef and an artist. There's a huge team of people with diverse skills who need guiding, coaching and leading. You're highly skilled at your craft, deftly bringing together solutions to the complexities of content, messaging, partnerships, production, people, talent… the list could go on. And you bring a creativity and artistry to conceiving and creating the whole event.

Events are not so much a team sport as a trust fall.

High performing teams – and I've been privileged to work with many in client organizations – need brilliant collaboration and an enormous depth of trust between everyone involved. That's where the magic starts.

Engaging the whole team upfront is a vital element in visualizing the journey and ensuring the team are engaged and excited.

How Hull City of Culture took people on a journey

Award-winning event producer Martin Green CBE is just such a master chef/artist combo.

And as the lines between what used to be called B2B and B2C – business and consumer events – blur, and as business, professional and consumer events and their characteristics merge, there's a lot to be learned from major consumer events.

Martin has a phenomenal track record as an executive producer of major cultural events: the London 2012 Olympic and Paralympic Games ceremonies, Hull UK City of Culture 2017, the Birmingham Commonwealth Games 2022 and the 2023 Liverpool Eurovision Song Contest on behalf of Ukraine.

As MD of Eurovision in Liverpool 2023 on behalf of Ukraine, Martin oversaw the entire delivery of the most successful Eurovision ever, winning a 2023 BAFTA for Best Live Event.

Martin reflects warmly on Hull's 2017 City of Culture programme, which he led, calling it '365 days of transformative culture.'[1] The initiative featured four cultural seasons, 2,800+ events across 300+ venues and attracted 5.3 million audience visits. Designed to change perceptions of Hull, once dismissed as a cultural backwater, the programme successfully positioned it as a vibrant, artistic hub.

The secret, Martin explains, was deeply connecting content with the people of Hull. While boosting tourism was a goal, ensuring the city's residents felt ownership was key. The project fostered a three-way bond between place, people and artists – some local, others from afar – ensuring Hull's untold stories were embedded in the work.

'You also want to ensure it's invitational,' Martin told me, 'Not patronizing. So in opening week we dropped an invitation through every letterbox in the city. Everyone is invited. You can never say you were not invited. Although you may choose not to come. The relationship is an active one; we know you'll see your stories all the way through it.'

This built enormous cultural confidence: leading to a 500% rise in gallery visits and 95% of residents engaging in at least one cultural activity. Seven years on, 2,000 volunteers still contribute. More than half the audience came from outside Hull, and 75% of visitors said the programme improved their perception of the city. That's both a transformation and a journey.

Exploring the power of storytelling

The participant journey is a story. To powerfully affect people you will want to craft a human story that connects with individuals: nudges them to choose to attend and enabling them to find their own path through the immersive experience on the day.

Professor and writer Joseph Campbell said, 'people forget facts but they remember stories.' When we find ways to both create a narrative around our event, and stories and journeys within it we make it powerful, personal – and truly engaging and memorable.

What can narrative models teach us about event stories?

Business and professional events have been on their own journey as events have become more sophisticated. I introduced the Event Evolution Model in the Introduction, and we know that in the last 30 years, gatherings have developed from product → service → experience → emotional engagement → transformation.

Successful events need participant emotional engagement. Ensuring that your gathering has a narrative structure helps make your event feel human and connect with participants emotionally.

The hero's journey

While psychoanalyst Otto Rank developed a hero pattern in the early 20th century, Joseph Campbell popularized the hero's journey in his 1949 book, *The Hero with a Thousand Faces*.[2]

His 'hero's adventure' is a universal paradigm. Campbell describes it thus: 'A hero ventures forth from the world of common day into a region of supernatural wonder: fabulous forces are there encountered and a decisive victory is won: the hero comes back from this mysterious adventure with the power to bestow boons on his fellow man.'

Or as we might say nowadays: the hero goes on an adventure, learns a lesson and returns home changed. This is often described as crossing the threshold; a journey from the known to the unknown, returning to the known, or a journey from the ordinary world (before you've had the gathering experience) to the special world (your gathering experience), returning to the ordinary world changed in some way.

The Participant Hero's Journey

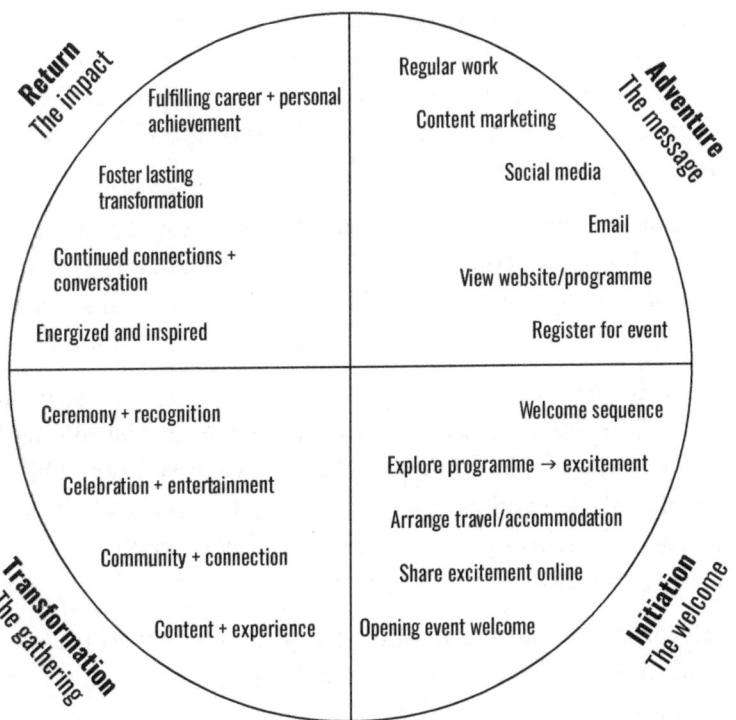

The Event Participant's Hero's Journey

Inspired by Joseph Pine's work applying these principles to brand experiences,[3] I have created the Event Participant Hero's Journey. This maps the participant experience from the call to adventure (receiving the marketing messaging), the initiation (the pre-welcome welcome discussed in Chapter 8), the transformation (the live-event gathering experience) and the return (the impact, your participants changed life and work).

The power of making the participant the hero of your event is game-changing. Participant-led event design will reap rewards.

Fear and greed

Robert McKee's *Story* is the bible for screenwriters and novelists.[4] He champions storytelling as a craft, and he focuses on structure, character and emotional impact. Unsurprisingly, he is both a powerful storyteller and phenomenal teacher; I attended his STORY Seminar live in New York in the early 2000s, and he was inspirational, witty and charged you $10 if your phone rang during the seminar. At least two people had to come to the front of the auditorium and hand him cash. And nobody present ever forgot the experience.

I took away some core ideas around story structure and how early you need to grab people's attention to keep them engaged. It has continued to inform my thinking about how events need an inciting incident – something that sets the story in motion.

McKee suggests there are only two key emotions – pleasure and pain. While it's possibly a slightly reductive model, it's useful to analyse how this thinking helps us as Chief Event Officers. Just like Black Panther activist Eldridge Cleaver said, 'if you're not part of the solution, you are part of the problem' – it's an oversimplification – yet still powerful.

Early on in my event education I was taught that in the events world there are two core emotions driving event attendance – fear and greed.[5]

Fear is pain – something's broken, and attending an event might fix it. Greed is pleasure – an opportunity awaits, and the right event can unlock it.

So residential landlords might flock to a conference on the implications of the new Renters' Rights Bill – fear. Or you might invest in a ticket for MIPIM, the world's leading real estate event, to access global capital to do business – greed.

Seven basic plots

Christopher Booker's *The Seven Basic Plots* systematizes all stories into these models: overcoming the monster, rags to riches, the quest, voyage and return, comedy, tragedy and rebirth.[6]

For gatherings, each of these models can serve as a potential tool to help us frame the story we want to tell about our event.

Dame Melinda Simmons, UK Ambassador to Poland, told me about how her team helped solve the ultimate quest at the 2005 G8 Summit in Gleneagles, where she helped secure a groundbreaking aid commitment for Africa.

First, she approached Sir Bob Geldof to support Live 8, a global series of concerts raising awareness about poverty. The event, broadcast to over 30 million viewers, ignited public consciousness and laid the groundwork for policy change.

The summit's purpose was clear: set a bold, transformative goal – in this case, making poverty history. Live 8's emotional resonance engaged the global public, creating momentum that the summit harnessed. The concerts connected audiences through music, while the summit, a more traditional policy-driven event, converted that energy into action.

Simmons described the importance of this dual approach: one event captivating hearts and minds, the other delivering concrete results. The team worked tirelessly to align messaging and build influential support. Just a week after Live 8, G8 leaders pledged to double aid to $50 billion by 2010, with half allocated to Africa.

The strategy? A clear purpose combined with a bold goal, compelling storytelling, influential advocates, and seamless alignment between public engagement and policy decisions helped the world feel that it had contributed to completing the quest. Or, perhaps, helped overcome the monster.

What can events learn from narrative identity?

Professor Dan McAdams teaches psychology at Northwestern University. He developed the concept of narrative identity, the idea that the internalized stories people craft about themselves shape their identity. McAdams identifies two primary narrative forms:

▶ **Redemptive stories** transform hardship into growth, revealing meaning through overcoming adversity

▶ **Contamination stories** portray positivity turning negative, diminishing life satisfaction, for example where joy becomes overshadowed by tragedy

Narrative identity applies to events, too. Contamination stories dull the energy of your event.

But redemptive stories, stories of hope, future success, solving the challenge, they're the magic. We all want our events to lead on redemptive narratives; speakers who talk of overcoming obstacles or set out the challenge to do so, workshops filled with problem solvers.

English particle physicist, author and former rock star Professor Brian Cox is a masterful storyteller. With a career spanning academia, stage and media, he was invited to open the 2021 UN Climate Change Conference, Cop26 in Glasgow.[7] He told me, 'I had two minutes. I had to work out what was the most powerful thing to say.'

He told the assembled world leaders that it's possible there's only one civilization in the Milky Way galaxy, Earth may be the only place where intelligent life exists, the only place where that life can bring meaning into an otherwise meaningless universe. We must consider ourselves and our world to be inconceivably valuable.

Or as he put it me, 'if our civilization is destroyed through deliberate action or inaction then we may be responsible for eliminating meaning in a galaxy of 400 billion suns, potentially forever.'[8] Quite a story. And giving the listeners an opportunity to turn it into a redemptive story.

What we're looking for as we create and craft our event narratives is for them to have redemptive patterns, stories and content that help participants overcome whatever commercial, professional or political challenges they may have and find deeper meaning.

The Transformative Journey Plan

Thinking through the three categories – individuals, organizations and sectors – and using your growing knowledge of storytelling techniques, start to consider what journeys your event will create for each category and the stories you'll tell about each.

⬇ You will use this to create a **Transformation Journey Plan**.

Stories and narrative are a powerful human driver: the writer Joan Didion says 'we tell ourselves stories in order to live.'

It seems to me that individuals and events that have mastered the art of storytelling know how to grab people's attention, to lead, to inspire.

When Steve Jobs was CEO of Pixar in the 1990s, he apparently stormed into a meeting and stated 'the most powerful person in the world is the storyteller. The storyteller sets the vision, values, and agenda of an entire generation that is to come.' Of course, Pixar went on to release *Toy Story* in 1995, and that launched one of the most successful animated movie franchises of all time.

We've all been mesmerized at events when a speaker who's mastered the art of storytelling has hundreds or thousands of people spellbound from the stage. I once heard Clate Mask, the founder of Keap (then Infusionsoft), the CRM and marketing automation platform, speak at a conference.

Sitting atop a bar stool highlighted by a single spotlight on an otherwise dark stage with an audience of 2,000 marketing executives on the edge of their seats, he shared his businesses origin story and turned his business model into a purposeful story which in turn launched a million small businesses, and it was magical. When you see someone at the top of their game, it's transformative. And let's face it – it wasn't anything obviously sexy – he was talking about database technology. But what a storyteller.

Conversely, we've all seen a conference room where the speaker has failed to seize the audience's attention, and the room has collectively got out its mobile phone to demonstrate its boredom.

As cognitive scientist and linguist Professor Mark Turner says: 'Narrative imagining – story – is the fundamental instrument of thought. Rational capacities depend upon it. It is our chief means of looking into the future, or predicting, of planning, and of explaining.'[9]

It's also a powerful means of connecting with the present when we join a gathering; it's often the stories that resonate and draw us in. Stories from speakers about the big ideas they'll share. Stories from previous attendees about how great it is (testimonials). Stories from partners about why they like the event (social proof).

Our skill as Chief Event Officers is to take this narrative imagining and help our participants feel the power of the event. A great start is to use the Transformation Journey Plan to map out the desired journeys for individuals, organizations and the sector that you are designing into your gathering.

How events can use narrative models

How do you turn this psychological understanding into a narrative 'shape' for your event?

Donald Miller leverages the hero's journey as the basis for a brand marketing script, his seven step StoryBrand Framework.[10] He puts it like this: 'A character has a problem, they meet the guide, who gives them a plan, and calls them to action, which ends in success. And avoids failure.'

Your event follows a classic story arc. The delegate is the Character with a problem – your event provides the answer. They meet you, the organizer (Guide) who offers a Plan – event attendance. The Call to Action? Attend. The result? Transformation.

Founded by three doctors and a pilot, The Risky Business conference emerged from London's Great Ormond Street Children's Hospital (GOSH) cardiac team's efforts to improve the transfer of critically ill children from surgery to the intensive care unit (ICU). Inspired by Formula 1 pit crews, they sought advice from McLaren and Ferrari, applying F1 strategies to cut non-technical errors by 40%. Their findings were featured in *The Wall Street Journal*.

Since 2016, the conference has explored defining moments in safety-critical industries like NASA, civil aviation, offshore oil and nuclear energy, and how healthcare patient safety can be improved from this shared knowledge. Speakers have included Tony Blair and those involved in the Grenfell Fire, Thai Cave rescue, London Bridge terror attack and Salisbury Novichok incident.

Applying the StoryBrand Framework, you might say this. A Character (a senior doctor) has a Problem – there are too many safety failures. Well hello, Risky Business founders (the Guides), who suggest a Plan – come to Risky Business and reduce your safety errors significantly. Success.

A strong event often revolves around a theme, distilled into One Big Question – the pressing issue everyone's tackling. Your strategy might be to help participants Overcome the Monster, guiding them to 'defeat the evil', whatever that means for them, their organization, or their world.

Make your participant the hero of your event

Conference marketing guru Marjorie Maws was my early career mentor, and her phrase 'don't tell me about your grass seed, tell me about my lawn' has stayed with me for decades. Our job as Chief Event Officers is to put ourselves in the participant, speaker, partner or VIP's shoes, and see events from their perspective. They are the main characters.

Or as British writer Alan Moore, a visionary who has reshaped storytelling through graphic novels, puts it in *V for Vendetta*, 'everybody is special. Everybody has their story to tell.'

Informa's market-leading trade show, TISE (The International Surface Event), connects buyers and sellers in the floor covering, stone and tile industries for networking, sourcing and trend insights. With a diverse mix of architects, designers, contractors, quarries, retailers, builders, importers and distributors, navigating this expansive marketplace can be a challenge.

So how do you find out if the show will deliver on your specific needs?

In 2024, TISE launched StoryBooks to guide attendees through the show, tailoring content, networking and opportunities to specific career segments.

Large, market-leading events unite entire industries – buyers, vendors, press and VIPs – making navigation overwhelming. StoryBooks simplify this journey, helping participants find their unique path.

What's brilliant is TISE's framing: the attendee as the protagonist. When I see myself as the event's central character, I feel valued, engaged and essential. Who wouldn't want to attend an event where they're the hero?

Calling attendees to adventure

Martin Green talking about Hull City of Culture describes the call to adventure being 'an invitational', that you honour your participants in how you communicate with them.

Is the marketing campaign the call to adventure? Can you create one narrative thread or one narrative journey thread for each type of attendee (think of the TISE event) and tell those stories throughout the campaign? Imagine how your attendees will feel knowing you have crafted an adventure tailor-made with them in mind?

Your event might incorporate literal adventure – climbing walls or early morning runs – to engage with the human side of your delegates and begin their event journey, with them as the hero.

It's not just about how you invite the participants; it's sometimes about the exclusivity of the invitation.

News Corporation's annual management conference brings senior executives together to explore media and geopolitical issues. A private event held in exclusive locations like Cancún and Hayman Island, no agenda details or external media access are available.

For senior News Corp executives, an invitation is a true call to adventure.

The only leaked agenda was from the 2006 Pebble Beach event, led by Rupert Murdoch, covering climate change, brand building, poverty in Africa, and Islam and the West.[11] Speakers included (an apparently almost exclusively male line-up of) Tony Blair, Al Gore, Bill Clinton, John McCain, Arnold Schwarzenegger, Bono and Shimon Peres, with Newt Gingrich and Nicole Kidman among the notable attendees.[12]

'It's not your standard cookie-cutter management conference where you only talk about business,' News Corp spokesman

Andrew Butcher said. 'The businesses we run give our people unique social responsibilities in their communities. The retreat is meant to provoke and broaden their perspectives so they return home more curious and informed about the world.'

Internal events like these have the capacity to create excitement; the exclusivity of inclusion, the elevation of the conversation and the stories people will tell on their return.

Crafting your event journey and story

With these narrative concepts in mind, now you are ready to craft your gathering's journeys and stories.

The first question is: where do participants start and end their journey? What is their starting state? How do you intend for them to be changed by the end of the gathering experience?

Explore this for the individuals and organizations involved in your event and for the broad sector. Make a huge list of starting and ending state for each relevant category. Curate the ones that resonate with your bigger purpose. Map these journeys for each category; you'll return to these later to sense-check your event design.

Next, take the journey to the next stage; what stories will your gathering tell?

If your event has history, then the stories of past participant experiences and how they were changed. Stories of who participants might meet, connections they can make, possibilities. Speaker stories of the ideas they'll share and the impact they're aiming for. Creative stories about the music, art and installations which will bring your gathering's purpose to life. Partner stories about relationships built.

⬇ These are your **Gathering Story Pillars**. They'll form the basis of your ideas for messaging and content marketing.

Contextualize the journey

You've thought through the journey and how you shape the narrative. With that in mind, let's look at your events differentiators.

You're asking the important question 'why are we different?' You likely have competitor events and divining your unique selling proposition (USP), how you differentiate yourself from other players, is important. And that will help you craft your UNP – unique narrative proposition.

Is yours the only event that brings together specific sectors or sub-communities? Is the breadth of attendees your differentiating factor? Do you have a policy perspective that you can't get elsewhere? An important outcome of finding your why is to establish why you're different.

Take the software as a service (SaaS) market. SaaS, accessing applications via the web, was once an innovation, now a business model. Salesforce, launched in 1999, is often called the first SaaS company, challenging enterprise software. Today, over 30,000 SaaS companies exist, making it a distinct and competitive event market.

It has all the hallmarks that attract event founders: a robust tech vendor supply chain, VC firms already in the market and a thirst for connection and deals.

Let's take a look at the events. SaaSTR Annual launched in 2015, off the back of a WordPress blog, and calls itself the '#1 Cloud gathering', drawing 15,000 attendees in San Francisco. France-focused B2B Rocks, founded in 2013, attracts 3,000 and evolved into Paris SaaS Week. SaaStock, launched in 2015 as a blog, brings 4,000 to its Europe event, plus US editions and an invite-only VIP SaaSociety retreat. SaaSiest, the newcomer, emerged in 2021 as a 'hobby project' in the Nordics and hosts 1,200 attendees. There are now around 10 SaaS events in Europe.[13]

Each fosters a strong community, offering newsletters and podcasts, aiming to differentiate themselves in this competitive space. Imagine you are a new entrant in the SaaS events sector; what difference and value do you bring to the gathering party?

Benchmark your journey against your competitors

I am not sure there are any sectors left without competitors – and if that is the case, there's probably someone watching your success right now and developing their new event.

I invite you to place your gathering thinking in context – ideastorming your competitor events is vital. You may already have a spreadsheet, and/or you may want to run a workshop, consolidating all the players.

Who are your competitors? Other event organizers and owners, corporates, associations, media owners, commercial conference companies, training providers. Anyone competing for your delegates'/sponsors' time – this might also be social media, apps, print media (what's left of it) or in mature markets, the vendor supply chain creating their own events.

In the new era of work/life balance, I've seen people put personal/family time on a workshop post-it note. You need to constantly be ensuring that your event is a good use of someone's time, especially if they have to travel, leave domestic commitments and juggle work priorities.

Entrepreneur leader Will Green from Apurimac Africa says:[14]

> *any business executives worth her weight in salt will know the large investment it takes to attend a conference. This includes time away from family and the work to catch up after the conference. The repeated pitches, the late nights and lack of sleep in overpriced hotels and uninspiring conference venues. The very thought of a conference can lead to an increase in personal anxiety.[15]*

John Battelle told me, 'Every single minute matters where you have an audience's attention. Wasting one of those minutes is a crime.'[16]

There's an implied promise when you invite participants to engage in your gathering. They are giving you their precious time and attention, and in exchange you give them value. There's an opportunity cost to attendance, and it has to be worthwhile. Just as exhibitors and partners consider the indirect activation delivery budget (creative, stand build, staffing, travel and accommodation) on top of whatever their direct investment in the show.

Think of it as an event value equation:

Event value equation:
Attendee time + attention + cost of attendance > value

Your gathering must deliver more value than the time, attention and cost participants invest. In a competitive landscape, it must stand out clearly, so that participants, partners and speakers instantly grasp its worth.

Understanding your event within its competitor set is key to achieving this.

Articulate your differentiators

The competitor data is one element, but the power is in your analysis. Complex and mature markets will likely have a whole cornucopia of event player categories, and you will need to decide the best analysis model to serve your ultimate journey/storytelling purpose.

It seems to me that a visual analysis model is the most accessible route. While some prefer a detailed report, I'm a believer in the one-page graphic summary.

Consider the two most important analysis factors – for example, which events are more content-led over sales-led? Where are events on a non-profit to trade show axis? Where do events sit on commercially led agenda versus a purpose-led agenda?

UK Tractor/Farming Market Competitor Map

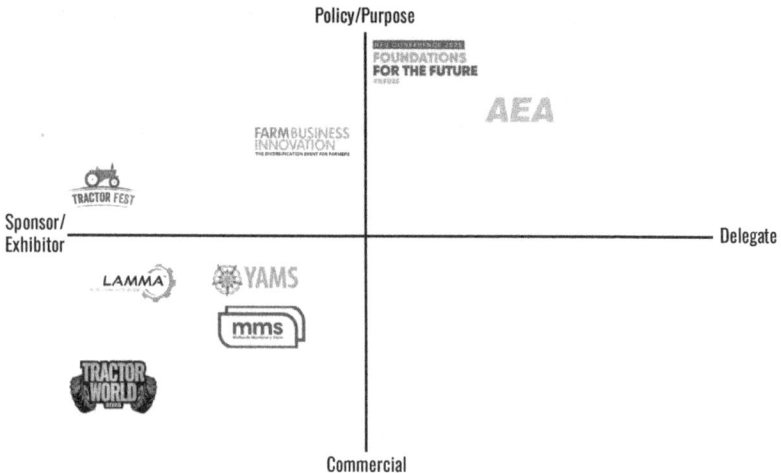

Event Market Competitor Map

Once you have your two questions, plot them on an X–Y axis – perhaps sales vs content and commercial vs purpose. Consolidate your thinking, then identify an open space where you can offer unique value.

⬇ You can use an **Event Market Competitor Template** to map your market and leverage that to explore your own **Event Differentiator Checklist**.

Consolidating the journey narrative

You've considered the first two questions – what's the transformation and what's the journey? The next step in the *Playbook* is to synthesize this thinking with deep thoughts around your event's true purpose, and from there create your Event Purpose Proposition.

Transformation. Journey. Purpose. The triumvirate of event strategy.

Chapter 3
Articulating the purpose

The last of the three 'why are you creating this event?' questions in the *Playbook* is (drumroll): how do you articulate the purpose of your event?

You've already created a Transformation Journey Plan, Gathering Story Pillars and Event Differentiator Checklist that articulate the transformation your gathering creates, the journey it takes participants on and the difference it makes. Bringing together the strands of thinking on the transformation and journey, the purpose thinking synthesizes those ideas, helping you move forward and create an Event Purpose Proposition.

Once you have this, everyone in your team – from the CEO, board, all the teams in your 'event orchestra' – your content, marketing and operational teams, delegate sales, PR, exhibition sales, frankly the build team – will totally get what the point is.

Successful events are often about substantial, diverse teams and having clear internal comms and external comms. This is a big key to unlocking superlative events where the whole team delivers. Developing a framework to define and express your purpose proposition and then formulating it with clarity can be a game changer.

Author and speaker Jez Rose says this: 'All too often in calls with clients when I ask what the point is for people attending the event, I hear: "That's a very good question; I don't think we've really thought about that".'[1]

We're aiming to change that and get clarity on your mission so that you'll be in a good place to create a superlative gathering.

Let's jump in and explore step three, how to articulate your gathering's purpose, and all the jigsaw pieces that make up the picture.

Know your purpose

Why are you creating this event?

'Because we always do our annual event in May' is not a good reason to convene. Nor is, 'but we've already reserved the venue', 'the CEO wants the event in three months', 'the users want the User Conference' (even if attendee numbers have been decreasing in recent years), or 'we need to do one more event to reach the budget / target'.

You've explored the transformation your event will achieve. How will the world – or your world – be a better place because of your event?

You've interrogated the participant-centric journey. Where do participants start and finish, and what change do they experience? How does this gathering compare to other events in your field? What difference does the event make and how is it different from others?

The next generation

The corporate world has developed its understanding of how businesses play their bigger part in our world, and there are board-level execs with remits such as Chief Purpose Officer and Chief Vision Officer.

There's positive sentiment around purpose; the rise of the B Corp – companies verified to meet high standards of social and environmental performance, transparency and accountability. Corporates are increasingly required to report on their CSR, ESG or environmental impact, and where it fits; this can be woven into a purposeful narrative linked to your gathering.

The tectonic plates of what drives recruitment and retention are shifting. In a world where employers are increasingly finding it harder to recruit and retain staff, delivering meaningful work pays dividends. According to analytics and advisory group Gallup,[2] employees who strongly agree that they know what their organization stands for are 3.7 times more likely to be engaged at work. By extension, this is also true about how events engage newer generations.

According to Deloitte, 'Gen Zs and millennials have long held a reputation for valuing purpose-driven work, and this year's study continues to support that idea. Roughly 9 in 10 respondents in both groups say having a sense of purpose in their work is very or somewhat important to their overall job satisfaction and wellbeing.'[3]

Businesses – and gatherings – are responding to this generational need for meaningful work. Now is the time to ensure that your gathering has a clear vision and purpose.

Formulating that purpose and vision to bring together the transformation and journey and create a depth of narrative and clarity of proposition will pay off through the rest of the event development process.

Money 20/20 launched in 2011 by industry insiders Anil Aggarwal and Jonathan Weiner and now has the strapline 'where money does business'; a powerful articulation that pinpoints the sector and the intent: the show is about doing deals and doing business.[4]

The 2024 content is headlined 'Purpose-Driven Stages to Illuminate the Next Big Idea'. And the opening pitch touches the transformation, journey/story and purpose high notes:

> *You'll leave the Money20/20 show with that indescribable feeling of not only seeing fintech celebrities and hearing what's now and next for the industry, but an immersive experience that was crafted to perfectly encapsulate the story being shared on stage.*

Let's jump in and explore how to synthesize your purpose.

'People don't buy what you do, they buy why you do it' – Simon Sinek

You may be one of the 67 million people who've watched Simon Sinek's 2009 TED talk on how great leaders inspire action, the precursor to his bestseller, *Start With Why*.

His concept of the Golden Circle is a framework explaining how great leaders inspire action. His model consists of three concentric circles: Why (in the centre), How (in the middle) and What (on the outside).

Many people and organizations operate from the outside in, starting with What they do, followed by How and rarely addressing Why. Sinek argues that truly inspiring leaders and companies start with Why – their purpose, belief or cause – before moving outward.

This powerful insight is equally true of events; establish your purpose to create inspiration for your participants.

Sinek argues that people don't buy *what* you do but *why* you do it and that this emotional connection builds trust and loyalty, making individuals and organizations more successful. Biologically, Sinek links this concept to the brain. The limbic brain, responsible for emotions and decision-making, corresponds to the *why* and *how*, while the neocortex processes rational and analytical thought (the *what*). By starting with *why*, leaders (and events) tap into deeper motivations and inspire action that transcends transactional relationships.

Ultimately, great organizational leadership is about inspiring others by clarifying and embodying a shared purpose, not just delivering products or services.

The same can be said of gatherings; your audience is inspired to attend because of the clarity of your shared purpose.

Gina Gill, former Executive Director of the UK Government Digital and Data Office, shared insights about the GovTech Summit – the premier event for public sector innovation since its 2018 debut in Paris, evolving through its 2022 edition in The Hague.[5] Initially a collaboration between Public (a GovTech fund and accelerator), The City of The Hague and the Dutch Ministry of the Interior, the event unites technologists, policymakers, public servants, founders, investors and academics to reimagine how governments operate in a modern and digital world.

It's now powered by Founders Forum (who partner with Informa on London Tech Week) and Public. Sometimes event brands, their history and ownership are a little like eighties rock bands forming and reforming.

The event has a clear purpose: a shared mission to bring transformational change to the public sector for the benefit of all citizens. In doing so, it has built a global community to supercharge the GovTech movement and leave an ever greater positive impact on the world.

Reflecting on the 2022 edition in the Hague, Gill told me, 'I like the big strategic thinkers; they lay out the art of the possible, where the world's going. Those big, interesting ideas that make you go away and think in terms of your own context, they're really powerful.'

The mix of startups and government technologists sparked genuine ideas. Gina said, 'I loved the pitch session – a bunch of entrepreneurs had three minutes to say "here's our thing and here's what we can do for the public sector". Was fascinating to see what real startups and SMEs [small- and medium-sized enterprises] could do. Short, sharp, insightful.'

Sam Guglani is a doctor (clinical oncologist in the NHS) and writer (author of *Histories*, a portrait of life in one hospital over one week) and the founder of Medicine Unboxed – a series of sell-out events exploring the intersection of medicine and society, seeking to inspire debate and culture change. Each event has a different theme: mortality, wonder, love or matter.

Open to health professionals and the public, it acknowledges medicine's moral, political and social challenges, demanding more than science – calling for deeper human engagement. Through the arts, it fosters wonder, reverence and connection, expanding understanding beyond knowledge alone.

Medicine Unboxed is an event masterclass in living your purpose.

Sam told me:[6]

> *The sessions feel like conversations or chapters in a book.*
>
> *That's what the arts do – throw light on stuff, interrogate it, the world and the whole business of medicine. Questions about our frailty and connectedness – the arts are lightning rods for those conversations.*
>
> *Funders always ask about impact – I say that conversation IS the output. Keeping those questions alive.*
>
> *I like the concept of enchantment – to move individuals, stimulating them both emotionally and cognitively, to a place of deeper enchantment, is outcome enough.*

I asked him what success looks like. 'More love, better care.'

More love looks like the joy and uplift people carry home – redemptive storytelling in action. It's your purpose made tangible. Marketing sells that promise; participants buy into it. Most get what they came for.

But there are always some events that fail to deliver.

When the purpose promise fails

Take the 2017 Fyre Festival; it was promoted on socials by influencers including Bella Hadid and Kendall Jenner, promising a luxury music festival on a private island in the Bahamas. The marketing was to-die-for – who doesn't want blue skies, sun and sand with luxury accommodation, gourmet food, stylish people and great music? Even if a ticket costs up to $12,000.

The 2019 Netflix documentary *FYRE: The Greatest Party That Never Happened* shared insights into the people and the process. The event was pitched as Coachella but way cooler, promising a 'cultural moment created from a blend of music, art and food'. This didn't materialize. As one team member later said, 'shooting the ad *was* the real Fyre Festival experience.'

Most of the 5,000 attendees complained about squalid conditions, lack of adequate water, lack of security, a tent city rather than luxury accommodation, lost luggage, no musical acts, event cancellation with guests on-site and the cheese sandwich that went viral – basically, chaos.

One attendee described it as 'closer to The Hunger Games or Lord of the Flies than Coachella.'

No surprise that there was a $100 million lawsuit days after the event cancellation, arguing that the organizers had known the event was 'dangerously underequipped and posed a serious risk to anyone in attendance', according to *The New York Times*.[7]

An FBI criminal investigation ensued; organizer Billy McFarland pleaded guilty to wire fraud, was sentenced to six years in prison and ordered to forfeit $26 million. This was followed up with a $2 million class action settlement in 2021.[8]

This is, of course, the worst case scenario, and one of the event's myriad issues was Billy not listening to or trusting his team who could see the disaster tsunami coming.

But a serious lesson in delivering what you promise.

Ikigai

I love the Japanese concept of Ikigai, which roughly translates to 'reason for being'. It represents the sweet spot where passion, mission, vocation and profession converge. Think of it as the ultimate life-work balance diagram:

▶ What you love (passion)

▶ What the world needs (mission)

▶ What you're good at (vocation)

▶ What you can be paid for (profession)

Where these overlap lies your ikigai – a fulfilling existence rooted in purpose and joy.

Unlike the 'hustle culture' mantra of chasing success at any cost, ikigai focuses on a balanced, meaningful life that benefits both you and others. It's not just about money or career but about

Your Personal Ikigai

Personal Ikigai Model

waking up excited for each day because your work resonates with who you are and your positive impact on the world.

Reflecting on this idea I came to my own personal understanding of ikigai:

- ▶ What you love – I'm curious about what motivates people and passionate about connecting them

- ▶ What the world needs – more opportunities to connect, the right meaningful events

- ▶ What you're good at – conceiving and creating gatherings that bring people together

- ▶ What you can be paid for – turns out I'm quite good at it and enjoying a successful career

My ikigai is community – this gives me a sense of purpose and something I reference when I'm invited to engage in a new project.

I am inspired and excited to support and explore different communities – helping my local park raise Heritage Lottery Fund money to renovate the historic gardens and keep the park open, supporting my kid's school with brand marketing and my clients' many fascinating niche areas of activity – and find new ways of convening people. My ikigai is community and the connection and gathering that means.

⬇ What's yours? Explore this further with the **Personal Ikigai Worksheet.**

Ikigai for events

The ikigai concept can be translated from the personal to the professional; I've formulated an event model to explore your event's reason for being, asking these four questions:

- ▶ What are participants passionate about (engagement)?

- ▶ What does your sector need (mission)?

> ▶ How does your organization add value (purpose)?

> ▶ What are your organization's expertise and community (transformation)?

⬇ Use my **Event Ikigai Worksheet** to explore these questions and help you and your organization establish that inner kernel of purpose.

The British Medical Journal – the BMJ – is one of the world's oldest medical journals, published by the British Medical Association, the trade body representing nearly 200,000 UK doctors.

With the BMJ's mission in mind (working towards a healthier world for all) the BMJ events team launched BMJ Future Health in 2024 – A digital health innovation gathering. Holly Edwards, who leads BMJ's events and partnerships, told me, 'it was designed

Your Gathering Ikigai

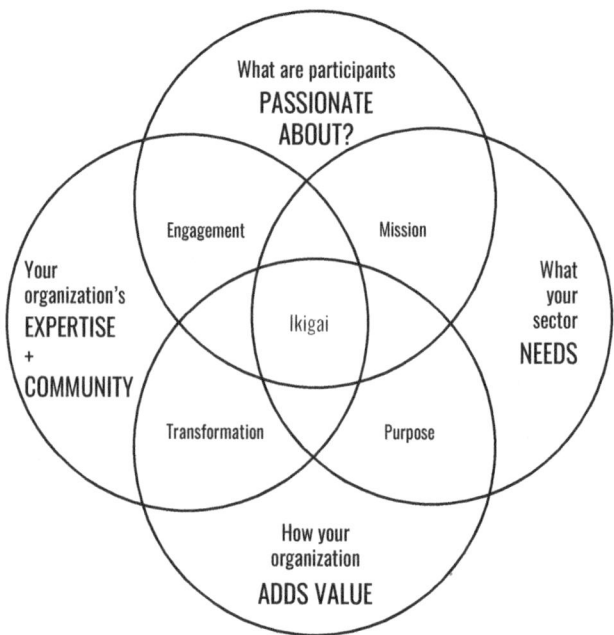

Gathering Ikigai Model

for sharing and interaction – building a community to achieve change.'[9]

BMJ Future Health's ikigai in this case is digital innovation – sitting in that sweet spot of the organization, sector needs and participant wants.

Swiss author and curator Bruno Giussani's career spans TED, *The New York Times*, the World Economic Forum and collaborations with CERN, among others. His expertise lies at the crossroads of politics, climate, economics and tech.

While at TED (for 20 years until mid-2024) Bruno co-founded and curated TED's climate initiative, Countdown. Not just another conference, it's an action-focused programme including conferences, designed to accelerate climate solutions.

Bruno told me, 'TED Countdown was primarily designed for impact. It was a deliberate choice to use all the available tools – events, TEDTalks, other forms of video content as well as coalition-building, to find solutions and amplify ideas to help confront climate change.'

The main event is the Countdown Summit – it isn't just about gathering 'an audience', it's about attracting the right people: scientists, technologists, policymakers, activists, entrepreneurs and artists.

Rather than passive listening, attendees exchange actionable ideas on tackling climate change.

As Bruno puts it, 'Communities need a clear social object to convene around – climate change is the most natural.' At Countdown there are talks but also brainstormings, connections with potential partners, funders and policymakers, as well as the projection of ideas through TED's global digital platforms.

The Countdown initiative includes 'Dilemma sessions', carefully curated events designed to look at some of the big 'knots' in the climate change space, 'where diverging positions have solidified into an inability to dialogue and seek how to undo them.

Climate change is the most pressing issue facing our planet, but it is prismatically complex, and exploring ways to unlock stalled progress is vital to ensuring a safe and just future for all', says Bruno.

> 'Most of us intuitively think of problems in terms of "choices": weighing alternatives and deciding the way forward. But many of those knots require us to consider competing values at the same time: that's a dilemma. It doesn't have an answer, but only ways to move things forward despite differences.'

Some of the ideas floated at Countdown have already attracted hundreds of millions in investment. The team (Bruno is no longer part of it) remains behind the curtain, letting the innovators take centre stage, but their work ensures their ideas don't just exist – they have an opportunity to spread and to scale.

How marketing straplines find deep purpose

Most organizations have a strap line. When those propositions speak to us, they create a relationship, something of an 'aha' moment. They understand me.

The power of getting the positioning right can be seen translated into business results.

For example, Nike's 'just do it' or Apple's 'think different' – calling out the characteristics of their customers, making them feel good about their drive and ambition or creative innovation.

L'Oreal's 'because you're worth it' has been putting the customer at the heart of the story since 1971.

EY says they 'shape the future with confidence'. Their purpose is defined as 'building a better working world.'

Airbnb's 'belong anywhere' encapsulates the feeling of community.

Money 20/20's 'where money does business' succinctly articulates that deals will be done.

Future Proof Festival's 'building the modern wealth management industry' implies community for the next generation.

Events are exactly like organizations – they have perhaps 3–7 seconds to grab the target audience's attention. In the world of short-form content it could be even shorter.

Shorter is better.

Our job is to leverage the best inspiration from the corporate world and use it to shape our strapline/mission/purpose.

When purpose meets events

Purpose has become so important that we increasingly see media owners and commercial event companies incorporate layers of meaning into their events.

Associations and corporates are more likely to have their vision and purpose more easily hardwired into what their gatherings do. Media-owned and commercial conference and trade show businesses have in recent years reinforced their events' propositions with 'bigger picture' impact and outcome stories.

Take the example of the FT's Global Banking Summit held in London in December 2024, convening leaders in investment, retail and corporate banking, policymakers, strategists and economists. The agenda included a range of conversations around risk, strategy, ESG, regulatory affairs, human capital, personalization and AI.

The keynote interview was Queen Máxima of the Netherlands, UN Secretary-General's Special Advocate for Financial Health, in conversation with *The Banker*'s editor-in-chief, Silvia Pavoni, on putting consumer financial inclusion on the global agenda and advocating for financial health as a key driver of sustainable and inclusive growth. Of course this is powerful; Queen Máxima is both something of a celebrity as well as having a formal role in Financial Health, and her involvement created many media moments while adding an extra layer of conversation to the proceedings.

Here's a more left-field example.

Kilkenomics, the world's first festival of economics and comedy was founded by celebrity economist David McWilliams in 2010. Dubbed 'Davos with jokes', it uniquely convenes some of the world's leading economists, journalists, financial analysts and sharp-witted stand-up comedians, demystifying complex topics like finance, geopolitics and human behaviour. Held in Kilkenny's medieval streets, it features informal panels hosted by comics who decode and debate serious issues with humour and clarity.

The festival sparks big ideas, fosters lively debates and builds connections, making economics accessible, relevant and even fun for everyone.

Reflecting on the Market Map model (which you will meet in the next chapter), this is – I think – unique positioning on the economics/comedy axis of your Market Map – whatever you put on the other axis. What's fascinating (and brilliant) about this event is that it has created its own unique space and a genuine purpose.

Strategist, educator and entrepreneur Mark Turrell founded unDavos in 2011 – a community-led series of interactive panels, talks and networking held alongside the World Economic Forum's Annual Meeting. The formal meeting welcomes around 3,000 attendees; unDavos is part of the expanding fringe ecosystem, now far larger than the main event.

Turrell told me his 'goal is to change the entire world for the better, all of it, at the same time'.[10]

The unDavos community was founded with a deep purpose; to create an inclusive, diverse and collaborative environment that promotes action-oriented learning and growth. It distinguishes itself from the World Economic Forum by focusing on grassroots participation, avoiding financial or political motivations, and striving for a human-centred approach to problem-solving.

Or as Turrell puts it, 'to connect the dots, at scale.'

How marketing value propositions help our gatherings

Brand marketing and event marketing are second cousins – quite a lot of shared DNA. Brands use value propositions as the ultimate overarching offering that adds customer value.

These simple statements, summarize why consumers would choose your product or service, the features and benefits, the overall experience, the problem your product/service solves and how you do it better than your competitors.

The focus is on how customers define your value, how you meet their needs and wants, and resolve their fears. Many brands call out their market, too.

Steve Blank, co-creator of the Lean Startup movement, co-founded eight Silicon Valley startups and now teaches entrepreneurship at Stanford University. He formulated this Value Proposition Framework:

We help (X) do (Y) by doing (Z).

So my local coffee shop might say:

93 Degrees helps Finchley locals to relax and connect offering great coffee and home-style Mediterranean food in a chilled, welcoming environment.

Such a succinct and useful model – and it has some transferrable relevance to gatherings.

Take the example of the FT's flagship banking event we mentioned earlier. We might write this:

The FT's Global Banking Summit helps influential banking professionals, investors, fintech innovators, policymakers and economic thinkers to shape the future of global banking by convening the event.

Community and connection

Gatherings are communities.

One big idea underpins everything about events, gatherings, conferences, summits, offsites, workforce events, client dinners – they're all about human connection and bringing people together for shared experiences. The events industry is built around relationships and trust – humanity.

Sometimes it's a pop-up community – that select partner group you gathered around the CEO to share her five-year vision.

Sometimes communities create events – think about every association you know.

EURORDIS (Rare Diseases Europe) is a non-profit alliance of over 1,000 rare disease patient organizations, hosting the European Conference on Rare Diseases.

Sometimes events create communities – Club Ichi, the club for B2B Event Marketers, founded by Liz Lathan and Nicole Osibodu, started out as a shout-out for event professionals in the Austin, Texas, area. Now it has 11,000 global members and 450 Insiders.[11]

John Battelle, founder of DOC and Producer of P&G's Signal event, said to me 'the thing about good events, you can't fake them, as they're expressions of community.'[12]

Taylor Swift's sold-out 2024 Eras tour seemed mostly focused on the friendship bracelets. Fans made them and swapped them with fellow Swifties at the live shows. What's it about? It might be the resurgence of 2000s styles, fuelled by Gen Z's nostalgia. But it seems to me that the friendship bracelets fostered a genuine sense of in-person community outside the online world and the chance to make new friends. Connection, the human desire for community.

The symbiotic relationship between events and communities is at the heart of what makes a gathering successful.

Strategies to design your event

The process of bringing together your thinking on the transformation, the journey, the narratives, the competitor context and the purpose and vision is variously called event design or event strategy.

However you describe the process, what's important is that you have core ideas about your gathering's deep vision and purpose at the heart of everything you do. What uplevels event professionals to event strategists and ultimately Chief Event Officers is the ability to think strategically around the value the gathering brings to the organization, individuals or the sector.

And with events increasingly being seen as the most important marketing channel,[13] Chief Marketing Officers and other C-suite executives may find that engaging in this process upfront will help create events that ultimately deliver desired business outcomes.

From value proposition to purpose proposition

I suggest that an Event Purpose Proposition has five elements.

G – the gathering
A – the audience
C – the content
D – how your event is different
O – outcome (the difference your event makes, it's purpose)

Event Purpose Proposition

(G – gathering) convenes (A – audience) to explore
(C – content) by doing (D – difference), aiming to
(O – outcome/purpose).

Let's take the example of David McWilliam's Kilkenomics festival. Here's how we might draft an Event Purpose Proposition:

> *Kilkenomics brings curious people to hear leading economists, journalists, financial analysts and sharp-witted comedians explore complex geopolitical topics in Ireland's medieval streets. The world's first economics and comedy festival aims to take economics, finance and geo-politics out of the conference to create accessible conversations for regular people. With jokes.*

Think back to the GovTech Summit. Their Event Purpose Proposition might look like this:

> *The GovTech Summit gathers pioneering technologists and founders, policymakers, public sector innovators, investors, and academics to explore AI implementation and public-private collaboration. An intimate, curated audience creates senior-level dialogue to move the dial on the digital transformation of public services.*

Canva's 2024 Canva Create transformed from an exclusive corporate keynote into a festival-scale event, drawing 3,500 in-person participants and 2.5 million online viewers. Essentially a user conference on acid, it showcased major product launches – including Canva Enterprise and AI enhancements – alongside keynotes, panels, workshops and community-driven sessions.

With 50 speakers across three stages – Create Stage, Design & Innovation Stage (curated by Fast Company) and Canva for You Stage – plus the Canva Learning Studio offering micro-sessions and expert consultations, the event blended high-impact content with premium production values, down to presenters' on-brand colour-blocked outfits.

A standout activation was the DIY Swag Shop, where attendees customized tote bags with Canva-branded patches. The event also embraced bold, unconventional moments – most notably, a rap about Canva Enterprise that went viral with 50 million views (not always in a good way). Canva styled out the 'playful moment', seeing it as an authentic brand expression.

Living up to its mission – empowering the world to design – Canva Create fostered a joyful, welcoming and inclusive community, uniting individual, SME and enterprise users in a celebration of creativity. Its success reinforced Canva's commitment to innovation and large-scale audience engagement.

So Canva Create's Event Purpose Proposition might look like this:

> *Canva Create gathers Canva creators – from small, mid-sized and enterprise organizations – to explore the latest product launches, hear world-class speakers and enjoy hands-on demos in a joyful, creative festival environment. Canva Create brings Canva's bold and unique brand to life, while empowering the world to design.*

RX Global's World Travel Market (WTM) has got its purpose position down. It describes itself as 'the world's most influential travel and tourism event'. That's already putting a stake in the ground.

Great copy and the invention of a WTM-owned ability 'Travelpower':

> *For 44 years, World Travel Market London has been the most influential three days it is possible to have in the travel industry. The place where ministers meet and global travel teams come to build their networks. And, if you're the 1 in 10 who work in travel, your influence is world-changing. So, how will you use your Travelpower?*

WTM has variants on this messaging, with the video using this language:[14]

> *Travel powers the world.*

> *Empowering whole communities, transforming individual destinies, from memory creators to policy makers.*

> *And if you're the 1 in 10 who work in travel and tourism, who make the connections that make the difference, travel is not just a job. It's world-changing.*

> *And your influence? It's called Travelpower.*

There are times when your gathering and its purpose are simpler. A small internal offsite for the team (increasingly a thing, post-pandemic). A small private dinner to connect… a thank you.

Moses Seitler, CEO of Screen Share, a non-profit supporting digital inclusion for refugees, shared details about *This Day Thank You*, an event hosted by This Day Charitable Foundation. Designed to celebrate grantees and partners, the event brought 300 attendees to a luxurious venue for a night of cocktails, fine dining and powerful stories from service users.

'It was glitzy but meaningful,' Moses said. He noted that non-profit work can feel tough, even discouraging, but the event provided a rare moment of appreciation and optimism. 'It felt like someone was on our side.' Unlike commercial awards, which often fail to live up to expectations – and require attendees to buy tickets – this event was purely about gratitude. 'Being treated like royalty was a new experience,' Moses reflected. 'It was about celebrating the sector and the work we do.'

Some events have simplicity of purpose – for example, corporate seasonal parties saying thank you to employees. A senior insurance industry executive said to me:

> *I remember the Howden Christmas party at the Natural History Museum in 2021, a huge party where no expense was spared to have a really good night out. Everyone felt that they were being rewarded for the year's work while at the same time being treated to something that was exclusive and fun.*

While these kinds of events can have a great impact on employee sentiment, engagement and ultimately the success of the business, corporates also need to be aware of the public messaging around investing in substantial parties and how it aligns with their corporate mission.

Articulating the power of your purpose

The Event Purpose Proposition helps you succinctly articulate your events proposition and the transformation it's designed to deliver.

Your consolidated thinking around transformation categories, your Transformation Journey Plan, Gathering Story Pillars and the Event Marketing Competitor Map helps you create your overarching event narrative.

With this strategic groundwork laid, you are ready to take this understanding into the second big question in the *Playbook*: who is the event for?

PART 2
WHO IS THE EVENT FOR?

Chapter 4
Mapping the stakeholders

We've explored the three 'why are you creating this event?' questions that support the strategic reasoning underpinning your event: what is the transformation and who is it for, what is the journey for those people and the stories we will tell about the journey, and what is our deeper purpose? We have understood how to synthesize those three conversations into an Event Purpose Proposition.

With this under our collective belt, we're well positioned to explore the first of the 'who is the event for?' questions.

Who are the stakeholders? And how do we understand how a complex market might fit together? It is this market understanding that will bring clarity for marketing (who to promote to), partnerships (who to sell to) and content (who is the audience and what content will excite them). The skill of market mapping helps visually understand this.

Who are the stakeholders?

Every event is a market. And every market has a range of stakeholders.

Why is an event a market? In economic theory, a market is where buyers and sellers exchange goods, services or information.

Most successful events are designed to convene a market; they bring together either buyers and sellers, or different subsidiary parts of a market to exchange ideas and debate. It's the breadth of voices and range of conversation that energizes those events. And it's often where business gets done.

Why does that matter to us?

Let's say you're a video game combat designer; you create the combat mechanics and systems that produce a satisfying experience for players inside a video game. Think *Street Fighter*.

So a combat designer is already a niche within game devs, the video game designer field.

An event that brings together *just* video game combat designers might be a lot of fun: shared experience, learning from others in your field, in-jokes about obscure Easter eggs, and combat and stealth behaviour. It's going to have two drivers: networking and content. Think back to the 5Cs in the introduction – content and networking is a webinar. Or perhaps a training course. Indie Game Academy does this well.

It's a niche field. As far as I know, there's no Association of Video Game Combat Designers, although there's very likely a Discord channel. They sit within the larger world of game devs (developers), and they attend events like GDC – Informa's Game Developers Congress,[1] the International Game Developers Association – IGDA events or Steel Media's Pocket Gamer Connects events. There's a myriad of game developer events.

They all share one characteristic – game devs and a whole range of other job functions in the videogame world come to learn and network, attracted by the great content. Sponsors, partners and exhibitors invest in the show either because they want visibility at the sector's go-to show or they can see that the content and overall show design will bring their customers. Big tech companies like

Meta and Google want to be there, as well as major game brands – Epic and Unity – and hundreds of other sponsors and partners.

So it's a marketplace. Most business events are some kind of marketplace: whether that's a huge exhibition hall, tabletop stands in the coffee area or an invitation-only micro-event where you get to meet just the right very senior people (prospects).

Nearly every event's market can be analysed through the lens of buyers and sellers. Typically those sellers have their own supply chain, often technology. Hardware, software, engineering, data.

And every market map is individual. While many markets have an obvious – and sometimes not-so-obvious – buy/sell dynamic, in a more complex or nuanced market, you may want to ask a different question. Rather than 'who buys, who sells?' you may ask 'who owns the power?'

How does the market flow?

Mapping your market helps you clarify market flow.

Content is often at the heart of business and professional events: those brilliantly curated conversations and experiences, and the speakers and talent having them (content), attract the delegates, the participants. And those participants in turn attract sponsors, partners and exhibitors. The content you have curated (the product) creates a product that the participants (the market) desire. Those attendees in turn become the potential customer (the leads) for your sponsors and partners. Sometimes, those sponsors and exhibitors are enticed into the event relationship with invitations to their *own* speakers – always with the caveat that it will be unhelpful to all if those presentations are sales-led.

These relationships sit in the context of the connections your gathering will design and create.

While this is the clear commercial model that underpins trade shows, conferences and media-owned events, it's helpful to

Event Market Flow

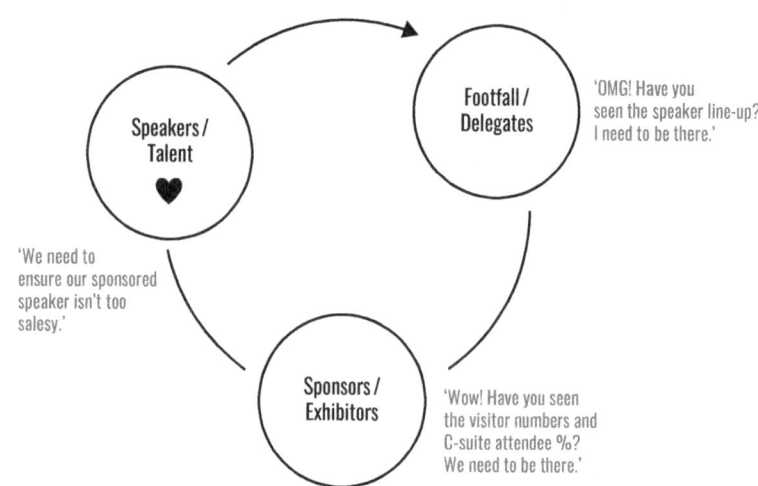

Market flow model

understand it to know which elements of it can be applied to a corporate, association or non-profit event.

Often, the differentiator for developing a meaningful non-commercial event is understanding how the market is structured.

Deutsche Landwirtschafts-Gesellschaft, DLG, the German Agricultural Society, was founded in 1885 by Max Eyth, and it hosts the biennial EuroTier trade fair in Hanover, the world's leading event for professional animal husbandry and livestock management. It welcomed over 120,000 visitors in 2024 from 150 countries, with over 2,000 exhibitors, and hundreds of co-located conference and professional events.

The content – those events – includes the International Cattle & Pig Event, The International Poultry Conference, Farm Robotix, International Conference on Ukraine/Moldova, China Forum, Animal Health Event and the Inhouse Farming Event.

So how does the EuroTier market flow?

Delegates – professional farmers and traders in cattle, pig and poultry farming, specialist livestock innovation and technology professionals – are drawn in by the vast amount of content. That content implies you'll be able to meet everyone you need to – it's the go-to event. They're enticed by conversations around animal welfare, sustainability, digitalization, AI, renewable energy, climate protection, herd management, quality assurance and smart farming.

Those 120,000 visitors are music to the ears of the 2,000 exhibitors. They know their customers will be there. So they sign up. Of course, there's an enormous visprom (visitor promotion) campaign to get delegates there, likely heavily led on the quality of the conversations and connections.

So, what is a market?

At its simplest, a market is where buyers and sellers come together to buy and sell.

It's your local town centre market where stall holders show their wares and you buy them.

Consider the International Food and Drink Event (IFE). The IFE brings together over 27,000 attendees (buyers) to meet over 1,500 exhibitors (sellers). They position themselves as 'the UK's ultimate business event for food and drink product discovery'. A market.

MCM Comicon has developed from a niche event in 1970 targeted at comics and science fiction fans. Now it's a global franchise and 'the premier popular arts convention in the world'. Join them for an epic three-day celebration of all things pop culture. It's a market, albeit a B2C market.

The UK franchise is owned by Reed Exhibitions, and it brings together buyers (fans) and sellers – comics, content creators, artists, illustrators, collectibles and collectibles kit, and all things pop culture and geek.

Adobe Summit is a market flipped on its head. CMOs and other marketing leaders and creators (buyers) come together to understand what Adobe (the seller) can offer them as its product suite develops. And they pay for the privilege. There's a supply chain of other advertising, consulting, design and technology companies who want to align themselves with Adobe, meet their audience, who Adobe has kindly convened for them, and build brand awareness and leads.

A market convenes all the players – market participants – and creates opportunities to connect and do business.

Mobile World Congress (MWC) is one of the world's largest conference and trade shows, with over 101,000 attendees in 2024 – describing itself as the most influential exhibition for the connectivity industry. Since 2006 it has taken place in Barcelona. In fact, the City of Barcelona has upgraded its transport and infrastructure off the back of its multi-year engagement with MWC. This partnership has helped Barcelona maintain its number four position in the ICCA City Rankings.[2]

Aside from the significant economic impact the show has on the local market of €550 million in 2025, there's the huge amount of business that gets started or signed at the show.[3]

Your event is a 'market', and the challenge is to get under the skin of which categories of people and organizations are on which side of the buy/sell line.

The power of visualization

David McCandless, the data visualization expert and author of the Information is Beautiful series has brought new insight into the art of visualizing data. He started out as a journalist but found that diagrams often conveyed stories and information faster and more simply. He tells a great origin story about his journalism career: when he was a kid he was obsessed with video games; he reprogrammed them, and this eventually landed him a column in a magazine. That's how he got into print journalism, writing about video games.

In his talks he explores an information-driven tour of the universe and considers visualization as a 'new kind of camera, thinking compositionally.'

One of the magic pieces of a Market Map is its simplicity and brevity – a one-page map over, say, a 30-page report. David says 'visualizing information is a form of knowledge compression.'

Our Market Map is absolutely about visualizing complex information, as simply and accessibly as possible. It also becomes a tool for the whole team to understand the market.

What's the benefit of mapping your market?

Conceiving an event is an act of creative leadership. You're not just creating a gathering – you're orchestrating an ecosystem. And for that, you need a Market Map.

Think of it as your event's big-picture brain: a visual, collaborative tool that captures the complex, ever-shifting dynamics of your market. Whether you're at a lean event startup or wrestling with layers of corporate sign-off, the Market Map speaks to everyone. No death-by-deck. Just one clear, accessible asset that drives understanding and action, and makes the insight land.

The Market Map is your ultimate comms and content Swiss Army knife. As a comms tool, it positions you as a market authority: if you can read the terrain this well, imagine the conversations you'll curate. As a content tool, a simplified version becomes endlessly deployable – across socials, content marketing and more – showing your grasp of the market while teasing the brilliance of your gathering.

Done well, it helps participants self-select. Who are they going to meet? If they're in TV production, will the networks be there? If they're in the ice rink market will the right ice surface treatment and sprinkler people be there? Your Map becomes a shorthand for relevance and ROI.

Because this is the core Chief Event Officer move: mapping the people who matter. Delegates. Sponsors and exhibitors. VIPs. Media. Knowing where the power lies – and putting it in the room. Mapping isn't admin. It's your superpower. Use it.

The principles of the Market Map

With that in mind, let's build your Market Map. Four core quadrants form the basis of nearly every market (although there may be others); buy side, sell side, must-haves and media.

There are four core audience types:

▶ **The Buy Side** – your delegates

▶ **The Sell Side** – the partners, sponsors and exhibitors

▶ **The Must-Haves** – vary by gathering; who needs to be in the room to make your event a success?

▶ **The Media** – need little introduction

Buy side   Sell side

Must haves   Media

Market Map Quadrant Grid

Every market is unique – so while you almost certainly need these four quadrants, there may be other, additional considerations, depending on your sector. There may be specialist areas specific to your market; in public policy-driven sectors there's usually a presence from government, in many scientific fields academia needs to be well represented.

The subtle interplay of these audience types is what creates the market, making connections happen and supporting business getting done.

How mapping articulates your market's drivers

Gatherings are where people meet, relationships get built and deals get closed.

However, there are dozens of event business models. Whatever conceptual or commercial model you're following – sponsor-led, delegate-led, trade show, content-led – you need to create a Market Map in order to understand your market.

I've worked on events where people actually do business – there's a day where deals get done and contracts get signed, and the whole sector is aligned to this timeline. At most events business definitely gets discussed – and lead generation and relationship building is a focus. And every event has a lounge or coffee area, soft spaces to talk business, make connections, explore partnerships. Modern commercial events often incorporate thousands of pre-planned 1:1 meetups, and the hosted buyer model has done this for decades.

In 1840, *Insurance Post Magazine* pioneered postal publications, guiding the UK's general insurance industry. To elevate its influence and revenue, Incisive Media enlisted me to create a new product to secure their position within the sector and develop a revenue-generating product to enhance their current suite of offerings.

In 2007, I conceived The Post Claims Club, an exclusive network for senior insurance claims and fraud professionals, then offering a quarterly, invitation-only forum under Chatham House Rules.[4] A select group of sponsors engaged subtly with attendees. Sponsors were limited to how many of their senior executives they could bring, ensuring the right balance of participants in such a small selective event. But they were (subtly) gaining access to the top customers we had convened for them.

This model has thrived, inspiring imitations across sectors and securing a significant revenue stream. Nearly two decades later the Claims Club brand, now under Infopro Digital,[5] has expanded into regular briefings, newsletters, podcasts and The Claims Club Summit – an exclusive closed-door event for the market's leading influencers.

The Hosted Buyer model is popular with many trade shows. The event organizer pre-qualifies the buyers as having budget and sign off. The buyers get to attend the conference/exhibition/trade show on the understanding that they'll attend a certain number of pre-booked meetings. Buyers get a personalized itinerary with well-matched suppliers. Where a buyer has a genuine need, it's a time-efficient way to get a ton of meetings done in a day or two and understand exactly what's on offer and make decisions.

Ray Bloom, founder of EIBTM (now IBTM) and IMEX, is considered the inventor of the hosted buyer concept, a key strategy that has helped the success of the shows.[6]

In the UK, Richmond Events leveraged this model, calling it 'strategic business forms' some 30 years ago. Their events happened on cruise ships – fun, exciting, but crucially, you couldn't leave. The hosted buyer element is a popular aspect of many trade shows; key decision-makers are hand-picked and hosted in exchange for taking meetings with vendors. When it's a good match, this is very powerful; buyers see all the vendors efficiently in a short time and suppliers get great meetings with qualified leads.

Your event might *not* be the location where people sign contracts with suppliers or agencies. But if you've understood your Market Map well, there should be ample opportunities to meet. It's likely to be the place where conversations are started, connections are made and ideas are ignited. Where leads are developed at the top of the funnel.

Trade shows are very explicitly about buyers and sellers. Your event brings the sector or industry to life. If you've got it right, it becomes 'the' meeting place, the must-attend event. You convene all the players, curate meaningful content and design an experience that creates the energy to propel the conversations.

At an event where I curated top-tier content, one of the senior government speakers said to me, as if experiencing the idea from first principles, 'this is great – my team can see all the vendors very efficiently in just one day out of the office'. That's copy that writes itself.

The corporate event model is sometimes more subtle. Corporate events typically have three main drivers:

- ▶ Capturing new audiences and building relationships (leadgen/pipeline)
- ▶ Adding customer value (user events)
- ▶ Driving business performance and growth (internal events).

Business is done more at the first type.

There are generational differences in every sector about *how* business gets done and conversations happen, but the principles are the same and it's beneficial to understand them.

Buy side/sell side

I started out working on marketing for financial conferences in the late 1980s. My MD was a phenomenal woman, Ros Oxley, with an enormous brain and a laser-like ability to analyse any market sector.

Perhaps it helped that she'd been a former City trader on the London Sugar Exchange floor. She taught me the basic principles of financial markets and how to apply those to analyse any market.

> ▶ **Buy side** refers to firms that buy or invest in securities, typically on behalf of clients; pension funds, asset managers, hedge funds and insurance companies. If you have a pension or an investment ISA, you're an individual investor – your fund managers pool your money with others' to invest in stocks, bonds and other assets on your behalf.

> ▶ **Sell side** refers to firms that create, sell, or trade securities; investment banks, brokerage firms and advisory businesses. For example, if a large corporation needs to raise capital, it may work with an investment bank to issue equity (stocks) or debt (bonds), which the bank then sells to buy side firms or investors.

If you are an association then it's likely that your members are on the buy side, and your supporters, vendors, suppliers or typical sponsors are on the sell side. Each market has its own complexity; I've seen chains of sell side suppliers who sell to each other up the value chain. Or markets where some organizations are both buy and sell side – with different job titles in the organization sitting either side of the line.

The National Bed Federation (NBF), a trade association, has represented UK manufacturers of beds and their suppliers since 1912. The NBF hosts the annual Bed Show, where bed buyers and retailers can meet the manufacturers, component suppliers and recyclers. For the NBF, the market model is inverted: members are the manufacturers (sellers) and the delegates are the bed buyers and retailers (buyers).

If you're a commercial conference company, trade show business or media owner then you're effectively a market maker. You are bringing together the buy side and sell side so that they can meet and transact business. And also connect, learn, be inspired, party, do yoga, go for a run, have a fascinating and uplifting experience.

Tech Show London, owned by Closer Still Media, is an award-winning trade show sitting at the heart of the convergence of the tech industry. Five co-located events covering cloud, DevOps, cyber security, big data and AI and data centres sit under the Tech Show London banner. Tech Show London is where senior IT people – Chief Information Officers (CIOs), Chief Technology Officers (CTOs), Chief Data Officers and their teams meet, learn and explore potential vendors, or meet up with existing suppliers.

At its broadest it's a trade show – exhibitors pay to take a stand, with over 400 stands in 2025. Some 100% of the revenue comes from the sell side vendors – exhibitors and sponsors – and there are just under 20,000 attendees attending free of charge. A huge amount of energy goes into the visprom, ensuring that the right level and quantity of attendees are on the show floor. Phenomenal content and great marketing attract them – the energy on the day is palpable. The Tech Show London Market Map might dig deeply into all the vendor suppliers on the sell side and build out all the categories of potential attendees on the buy side.

If you're a government or policy organization then you're likewise a market maker. You're bringing together all the players – for a specific objective you have in mind. Could be policy. Could be business – think Trade Missions.

Take the UK Department for Business & Trade's 2024 9th Pension Funds Mission. Welcoming a dozen finance professionals from Brazil, it was designed to develop lasting relationships between Brazilian pension funds and British financial institutions.

A UK Trade Mission expert told me, 'some only need a small number of well targeted contacts on a mission – a couple of deals makes a huge economic impact.'

If you're a corporate or big brand, then you could be either a buyer or a seller. In the Adobe Summit example above, Adobe is a seller, bringing together its buyers but also connecting those buyers with Adobe's own partners and supply chain. In this case, you're a brand with such equity in the market that you have the power to convene buyers and other sellers want to join you.

Or maybe you're an international consulting firm convening the global partners for the annual strategy review. In this case your buyers and sellers are both internal. The 'buyers' are the partners, and the 'sellers' are your internal marketing/strategy team who are pitching the ideas in an attractive, engaging fashion. Selling the strategy.

Creating your Market Map

When you gather to map your market, there are a few questions to ask before you kick off.

- ▶ Establish geography upfront. Is this a national, regional or global event?

- ▶ If your event has history, prepare the data analysis before you start. Look at the job functions, types of organizations, geography, seniority. Analyse who's already attending your event to help you extend your thinking into who's missing.

- ▶ You don't need me to tell you that with the right sophisticated AI prompt you can get an elegant analysis of your enormous datasets answering your big questions ahead of time.

⬇ Let's review the **Market Map Template**:

You may want external facilitation support. An expert facilitator can both elicit more nuanced responses as well as ask tougher questions that you as Chief Event Officer may not want to ask yourself.

Digging deeper into the four quadrants

This Market Map Workshop helps you look deep within your market in order to map your ecosystem. This supports your understanding of the varied players in your world; and any other unique considerations your market has.

In creating a visual Market Map consider these four core quadrants:

- ▶ Buy side – delegates.

Buy side		Sell side
Must haves		Media

Market Map quadrant grid

They may be paying to attend, although not in every business model. Some delegate categories might also work on the sell side, or there may be different job titles from the same organization on different places on the Map.

Think through the various categories or organization. It can be helpful to group them together, co-locating them on your Venn diagram.

If you're a corporate, your main client group will probably be the core of your buy side. If you're an association, your core members are very likely to be at the heart of the buy side. If you're a media owner, your largest delegate group will likely be on the buy side.

▶ Sell side – sponsors and exhibitors or vendors.

Where you have them, they often underwrite the event running costs through commercial packages. What they are really paying for is access. Access to the 'buy side'. You are creating a market, and they are leveraging that for their commercial or strategic purposes.

Typically organizations with a product or service or information / data to sell to your core audience. These sponsor and exhibitor organizations may well have their own supply chain, and it can help to reflect this on your Market Map.

Start by listing the main classifications for vendors. With an existing event, you'll probably already know this. Whether existing or new, explore what new categories of vendors are appearing. AI? Sustainability? For example, you may have different categories of vendor along the lines of software/hardware/consulting/funding.

▶ Must-haves – who are the big names or organizations that you need in the room for the important conversation to happen?

The must-haves help make your event both successful and the 'got to event'. Did you hear that Deepak Chopra and Queen Latifah were at Cannes Lions in summer 2024?

Start by listing out categories: government or policymakers? Trade bodies, academia or types of organization that are specific to your sector? It's helpful to include names of specific people, job titles or types of people from particular organizations.

You'll use this as part of the process to build out your VIP Invitation List later, so be as specific as you can. You might include 'CEO's private dinner list' or other internal listings or groups you have. Board member contacts are vital here – you might include '10 × invites for each Board member', for example.

▶ Media/press – do you want a media presence? Most events do. I'm increasingly seeing the power of the 'long tail' of thoughtful PR storytelling around events, so it's absolutely worth considering.

The right media in attendance will amplify your messaging and stories, and those of your speakers and sponsors. These are the organizations that you will build your marketing and PR plan around; the people you'll partner with and co-promote.

Map out all the media players: specialist trade press, websites, Substacks, newsletters, podcasts, influencers, national and regional media, Twitter/X and Instagram. Consider niche networks and communities across a variety of channels such as WhatsApp and Slack.

Every market is different

While the Market Map Workshop is a tried and tested process, every market is different. Before you gather to map, you may want a short brainstrust with a trusted advisor to explore and verify the shape of your Market Map.

Market Maps in scientific and medical research sectors often need additional spaces for academia. Market Maps in complex global markets need to find a way to demonstrate both geographical reach and multi-level vendor supply chains. Market Maps for corporates can focus heavily on the 'buy side' and very little on the 'sell side'. Conversely, I've seen corporate Market Maps that build out sophisticated and layered distribution networks. In these cases, the market mapping exercise can help shape the event design, with suppliers becoming a crucial part of the event.

Some Market Maps have complex relationships and connections that you may need to explain visually and will need more space for.

Plan ahead for this.

What to include in your Market Map

You need to consider three levels of information for the companies on your Market Map:

- ▶ Type of company
- ▶ Example company
- ▶ Job title(s) or functions of people at those companies

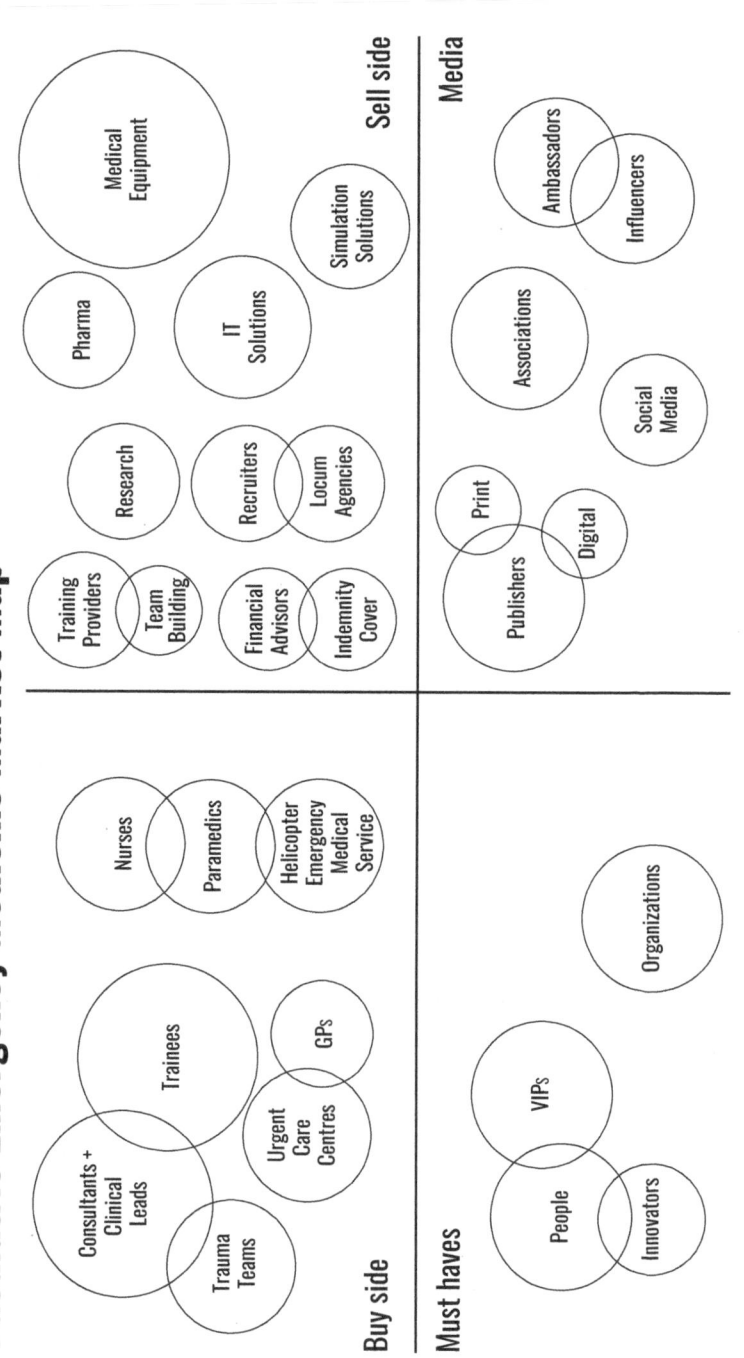

Market Map example

Example companies are useful to research related companies further.

Job titles and functions are useful to help you explore media that relate specifically to them.

Sometimes, the most useful niche marketing channels surface during this exercise. Make sure you capture them. If one of your board is in a WhatsApp group of CFOs in media companies and you're planning the Media CFO Summit, that's pure gold.

The Market Map helps you map your unique market – there's an example on the previous page.

Building engagement and leveraging value

The Market Map is not a 'done and file' exercise. The aim is to create a living document that helps everyone in the organization and event team understand the event market and their role in creating and delivering the gathering.

After the workshop, reflect and summarize. You'll also want to socialize the thinking around the organization. You might lead a slot in different team meetings across the organization. You might facilitate a session on the next team awayday.

You'll almost certainly want to reflect on it more fully with your full events team, exploring any gaps or missed opportunities.

Your completed Market Map is a powerful tool. Display a huge poster in your team area. Share it digitally with the team. If you're in a competitive space, make sure it stays inside your organization. The depth of insight and expertise you have collated would be something your competitors might really enjoy.

Are there other ways to use the Market Map? Absolutely. If you're working on a launch event, or in a new sector, you might use a simplified version as a branded infographic as part of your content marketing strategy.

This might demonstrate the lay of the land in a new or emerging market; giving the market a sense of its topography is very powerful. Alternatively, it might showcase your depth of insight in a newly launched show. Your new show or event will ideally have a unique differentiating factor, and this might be something you can bring out in your marketing version of the infographic.

Leveraging your Market Map to articulate your purpose

When you collate all the information from your Transformation Categories Grid, Transformation Journey Plan, Event Story Pillars, Event Purpose Proposition and Market Map into a Single Source of Truth, you have a core strategy document that can move you forward to the next stage.

You're four steps into the Playbook Process.

You've explored the transformation you're aiming to create: for individual attendees, for your organization and for your sector.

You've considered the journey: what is the starting and ending point for your participants, what journey will you take them on? This helps you begin to shape the narrative, the stories you'll tell about your gathering. As part of this thinking you've looked at your competitors and established how your event is different. There are a lot of events. Your gathering needs its USP, to demonstrate both how it's different and what difference it makes to the world.

And now you've synthesized much of that thinking about your market and the transformation and journey they're looking for into a Market Map which pins down all your stakeholders and where they sit.

You're in a perfect place to explore how you share the message about your event.

Chapter 5
Amplifying the message

You've worked through the first four strategic steps of the *Playbook* – Transformation – Journey – Purpose – Stakeholders – and you've mapped your market so you deeply understand your world and all the players.

These four steps are designed to clarify your strategic thinking and you've walked away with insight on the stories you want to tell, a Story Grid, Event Purpose Proposition and a Market Map.

With these in hand, the next step is to understand how to share the message of your event and how this can differ for the four (or more) core audiences you outlined in your Market Map:

- ▶ Delegates
- ▶ Sponsors and exhibitors
- ▶ VIPs
- ▶ Media

What questions do you need to ask in order to amplify the message and craft an Event Messaging and Marketing Strategy that delivers on your purpose?

In the following chapters, we'll explore the strategy and thinking that underpins the next stages of your *Playbook*: marketing, content, experience design and crafting the welcome. Later, we'll look at evaluating the impact of your gatherings and explore how events are becoming elevated to conversations around the boardroom table.

We will shift gear slightly for the next steps, sharing experience and insights on some of the strategic questions you'll want to ask in order to develop a cohesive strategy, which you will then want to develop into your own, specific, action plan.

You have your Event Purpose Proposition and Market Map in hand – let's get the message out there.

What's the Messaging and Marketing Strategy process?

This chapter walks you through the Messaging and Marketing Strategy process, guiding you with effective ideas to reach your four core audience types from your Market Map (delegates, sponsors and exhibitors, VIPs and the media).

First, we're going to explore the four core audience types and their differing requirements. You've got your Market Map completed, which helps you understand your audience – who they are (job titles) and where they come from (organizations).

Next, we'll ask, what's the best way to reach your different audience types? This will vary, depending on what market sector you're in. How do you tell the right stories to engage partners, sponsors and vendors? What's the best strategy to ensure your VIPs say yes to the VIP invitation?

We'll take that core understanding and use it to curate your audience. Messaging and marketing strategies need targets and your audience curation process will give you a laser focus on exactly who you want in the room(s) on the day(s).

The Audience Curation will help guide you as you explore strategies to reach your four core audiences.

Before we explore the core audience types further, there's one final step. Building on the Story Pillars and Event Purpose Proposition we explored in Chapter 2, you will build an Audience Messaging Grid, mapping out which stories will resonate for which audiences.

The power and challenge of event marketing

Strategic event messaging and marketing can make or break an event. Poorly planned gatherings thrive with great marketing, while brilliant concepts fail due to weak promotion. Investing in marketing at this stage is crucial, especially in competitive sectors.

This chapter explores some big themes: targeting individuals over job titles, the impact of shorter lead times, social media challenges, content marketing, B2B consumerization, sponsor outreach and crafting a media plan that extends your event's impact long after it ends.

Let's do this. Time to tell people about your event.

Who is the message for? Understanding your four audience types

Your four core audience types reflect the audience types already explored in the Market Map. Your message telling the stories about the purpose of your event and the difference it makes to the world is (typically) designed to reach four core audiences. They each need differentiated content and approaches to maximize the reach.

This is the perfect time to refine the Story Pillars you created in Chapter 2 and the Market Map from Chapter 4 to bring it all to life as you explore your gathering's messaging.

▶ Your delegates attendees are your core audience, for your event, or the footfall for your show. They're largely busy, with overflowing inboxes, DMs and socials, and so finding engaging, attractive and personal ways of reaching out to them is vital for your event's success.

▶ Your sponsors or exhibitors if you have them, may well be a core group underwriting the success of the event. A 2025 research report[1] found that '37% of organizers attribute 40–60% of their event revenue to sponsorship deals.'[2] They're as busy as your delegates, and if they're decision-makers on big budgets, possibly more so. Create a nuanced and sophisticated strategy to both reach and connect and share the value they'll receive for engaging with your event.

▶ Your VIPs and must-attends are essential – without them, the event doesn't happen. If the Chief Scientist of the WHO is key to a health policy discussion, you need a strategy to reach and invite them. We'll explore how to build and connect with your VIP list.

▶ Media help both promote your gathering and – crucially – ensure your event lives on after that final round of applause, dance performance or live poetry. Your comms plan helps deliver your event's long tail and evaluate whether you delivered on your purpose.

As you review these categories, you may identify new ones of your own – consider their specific needs and how they differ.

Curating your audience

The art of audience curation is deciding upfront who you want in the room on the day. This gives your marketing team strategic direction; they know exactly what they're aiming for.

While I hear many clients saying 'we want 500 people in the room' or 'this is for our top 100 clients' what does this really mean?

Do you want 500 delegates? 500 clients? Speakers? Will speakers get guest tickets? What about your team, VIPs, key clients, and commercial partners? Can sponsors and exhibitors bring guests? Do marketing partners promoting the event get a seat? What about board members, executives, investors – how many tickets for them? Can senior stakeholders help build a VIP list? How big will it be? Will press be invited to amplify your event's purpose? And when the inevitable comp requests come in – how many are you prepared to give?

For example, a think tank conference for 600 participants, designed to cover costs but expand the organization's network, might have 200 paying delegates, the balance made up of policymakers, government, business leaders – all the target markets the think tank is looking to expand into.

Or a confex organized by a commercial conference company for 600 participants, with a profit imperative, underwritten by the exhibitors and sponsors.[3] This event is about convening the audience that the exhibitors and sponsors want to meet. There may be 100 paying delegates, plus a curated audience made up of the ideal sponsor audience, plus the right VIPs, speakers, guests and the trade press. Fewer paying delegates, more partnership revenue.

Map your audience categories at this stage. Begin with the different groups of people you ideally want in the conversation. While this is different for every event, the core categories are likely to be something like this:

- ▶ Paying attendees (if you have them)

- ▶ Complimentary attendees
  - ○ Team allocation
  - ○ Supported access places/lower middle income countries
  - ○ Students
  - ○ Early career professionals

- ▶ VIP list
  - ○ Key stakeholders/ambassadors

Curating The Audience

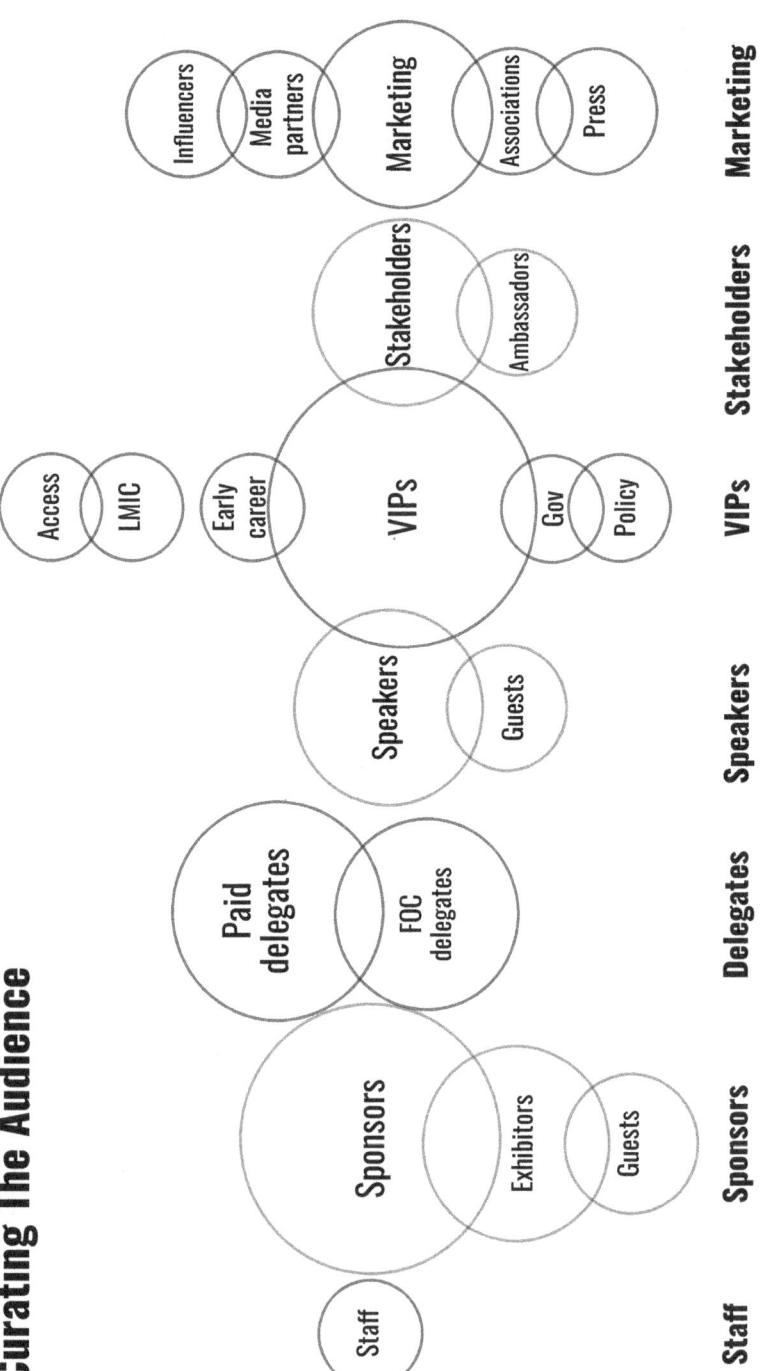

Audience curation model

- ○ Clients and potential clients
- ○ Industry leaders
- ○ Government/policy

- ▶ Sponsors
  - ○ Sponsors
  - ○ Exhibitors
  - ○ Sponsor's guests
  - ○ Exhibitor guests

- ▶ Speakers

- ▶ Marketing partners
  - ○ Press and media
  - ○ Associations
  - ○ Influencers

- ▶ Your organization
  - ○ Team
  - ○ Senior leadership team
  - ○ Board

⬇ Your organization will have its own objectives and its own market needs, and this is the ideal time to reflect on these as you build your own **Audience Curation Grid.**

As you curate your audience, you'll work across your organization – like the conductor of the event – liaising with sales, business development, field marketing, membership, customer service and, of course, engaging the board to ensure all the right strategic relationships are being considered.

Is there a Key Account target list you'd like to add to the VIP list? Are you seeking new members and are offering complimentary member tickets as a top-of-the-funnel activity? Do you have subscribers you'd like to incentivize to attend? This is the time to reflect your overall strategy and get it down on paper.

This is your list – build it out to reflect your ideal, wish list audience and the calculate how many of each category you're seeking.

If you have a commercial profit/surplus imperative this is the time to add revenue information for each category, so you can sense-check whether this strategy meets the commercial event targets.

	Ticket	Target
FOC	VIP complimentary tickets	100
FOC	Major stakeholders	50
FOC	Staff	35
FOC	Sponsors	75
FOC	Speakers	75
FOC	Guests	50
FOC	Access fund	100
FOC	Press	40
FOC	Partners	40
FOC	Influencers	20
PAID	Category 1 – paid tickets	150
PAID	Category 2 – paid tickets	100
PAID	Category 3 – paid tickets	90
PAID	Category 4 – paid tickets	75
	Total	**1000**
	(Total paid)	**415**

I often see organizations with broad audience data but lacking the refined insights that sharpen strategy. Skipping this crucial step can undermine your marketing impact.

With an understanding of your core audiences and your Audience Curation Grid in hand, you're ready to explore the messages to craft for different audiences.

Crafting your core messages for different audiences

Your message and marketing activities will vary by audience; the strategic skill is to clearly differentiate them.

Who are your core audiences?

Here's where you synthesize your Market Map and summarize the audiences you're targeting.

We talked about Advertising Week and its sector transformation back in Chapter 3; founded in 2024 in New York and now a global series of events serving the marketing, media, technology and culture communities.

Global President Ruth Mortimer talked to me about their audience analysis; there are five clearly defined audiences:[4]

- ▶ Brand marketers
- ▶ Creative agencies
- ▶ Media agencies
- ▶ Tech companies
- ▶ Media companies

What's fascinating about this audience analysis is that while each audience is clearly defined, they also have symbiotic relationships with each other. It's a beautiful, complimentary audience setup; the creative agencies and media agencies appeal to the brands; brands are also buying tech. Media owners want brands and agencies to buy advertising. Everyone wants to get into the media outlets.

This is the mark of a successful event with a lengthy history yet constantly developing – a laser-focused clarity on the market combined with a total simplicity of analysis. Plus a well-defined market where each sector has a spiders' web of connected relationships with each other.

VivaTech, held annually in Paris, is another event with a connected web of sector relationships.

Founded in 2016 by advertising company Publicis and France's first daily financial newspaper, *Groupe Les Echos* – the perfect partnership for vibrant branding and excellent media coverage.

VivaTech positions itself with 'Where Business Meets Innovation' to 'accelerate innovation by connecting startups, tech leaders, major corporations and investors responding to our world's biggest challenges'.[5]

Convening over 165,000 attendees, 13,500 startups, 3,500 exhibitors and 3,200 investors, VivaTech is Europe's biggest startup and tech event.

The landing page takes you directly to the 'here's why you should attend' page, and it clearly outlines the five categories the event is seeking to attract, with a message for each:

▶ Attendees – be part of Europe's biggest startup and tech event

▶ Startups – take your startup to the next level

▶ Exhibitors – get business done

▶ Investors – investors at VivaTech

▶ Media – the next hot story is here

This is a marketing and messaging plan writ large – total clarity on who should attend and why.

Talking to your audiences' authentic selves

'Authentic' was Merriam-Webster's 2023 Word of the Year. People want to bring their true selves to work – and to events – without hiding who they are.

As people bring their authentic selves to work, and events focus on emotional engagement, understanding attendees as individuals is a powerful marketing tool.

Post-pandemic, many events *are* where work happens. Hybrid work limits in-person connections, and video calls lack the complexity of human interactions. Major industry events now double as team meetups, especially for distributed or global organizations – an offsite-at-event model. And an opportunity for you to sell a team meeting room as part of the group package.

This shift highlights the requirement to understand attendee needs. Whether escaping the office or home workspace, events offer a mental refresh. Even with laptops in tow, attendees gain emotional distance from daily routines – perhaps even setting an out-of-office reply.

Connecting with other participants on a personal level deepens their experience. Participants will leave your gathering with an increased sense of authentic meaning if they made it personal.

Whether through networking, opportunities to do a sunrise salutation or dance the night away, events that recognize and cater to individuals create lasting impact. The key? Speak to delegates' *real* selves.

Participant Persona Messaging Grid

We've explored the four or more audience types, developed a nuanced approach to audience curation, explored your audience in depth, building a clear list of all the types of participants you're targeting, and we've reflected on reaching our audience's authentic selves.

First, there was demographics – raw data – then psychographics – internal attitudes and values. These marketing tools are combined in Participant Personas – a powerful tool to define your audience, their goals and their motivations for attending.

This is unique to every event. Slice and dice your audience universe any way that works for your gathering. Will you explore your personas based on the delegate/sponsors and exhibitors/VIPs/media model from the Market Map and the different messages you want to share with them? Are there additional persona categories – such as speakers?

Or more likely, your delegate/attendee audience is made up of different sectors with different needs.

The London Conference, hosted by the Centre for London, unites leaders to tackle the city's challenges. Its programme aligns with five research pillars – places, people, prosperity, power and planet – aiming for a thriving, decarbonized London. Attendees span local and central government, the private sector – including property companies, third sector, civil society and academia. The Centre for London marketing team might develop Participant Personas for the people in each of these sectors, identifying their goals, challenges and preferred media channels.

Reflecting on the VivaTech example we explored earlier, it looks like they've created Participant Personas for attendees, startups, exhibitors, investors and media, with a journey for each.

⬇ How do Participant Personas work? It helps to personalize them, create a fictional character for each of your personas, using the **Participant Persona Messaging Grid**.

Work through your Market Map and Messaging Grid and establish the core participants – their job titles and organization category. Explore more deeply their motivation, likes and dislikes, communities. Socialize this with your team to ensure you've covered the market. These are the people you want to reflect deeply on to ensure that you understand exactly what messaging you intend to send to each persona.

Tone of voice

Your event has its own unique personality, and in an overwhelming marketing messaging world, your tone of voice helps you communicate that. If you're still writing your copy in a faux formal business voice, I'd invite you to rethink.

Consumer brands have individuality and character. Think about Duolingo and its brand mascot Duo – the green owl. Duo is playful, encouraging and slightly humorous, bringing the brand's values to life.

The same for your gathering. Explore your gathering's voice (its unique perspective) and tone of voice, how it communicates with all your audiences. This is everything from word choice, emotional tone and communication style.

Your strategic thinking from the transformation, journey and purpose work will help you articulate what makes your event unique, its core values and from here you can establish what your tone will feel like.

User experience experts Neilson Norman have a model of the four dimensions of tone of voice, where each one is a spectrum:[6]

- ▶ Formal vs casual

- ▶ Serious vs funny

- ▶ Respectful vs irreverent

- ▶ Matter-of-fact vs enthusiastic

Creating an engaging brand

Your event brand is how you communicate the purpose of your event to your audience in a strong, speedy and visual way.

The brand is made up of a number of elements: the event name, a strap line / mission statement, a strong visual look and feel and its associated brand language and clarity on tone of voice. These fundamental elements can then be applied consistently and creatively to the very many assets you'll create: website, email, online ads, socials, onsite branding… the list goes on.

Received marketing wisdom tells us consumers (participants) have around 3–7 seconds to form an impression of your brand – and on social media this can be less. So having a strong purpose and visual identity is vital.

You might have a big team and/or a tech stack that creates all the ultimate assets, so building all this information into your Event

Brand Guide, a single source of truth on everything related to your gathering's brand will simplify the process down the line.

Because all our participants – and us – are consumers, bombarded daily with marketing messages, the brands we create for our gatherings need to grab people's attention, and for annual events, look like an old friend popping up to say 'hi, will we see you this year? You don't want to miss this.'

Take the events industry itself and some of the larger events that service it (and other allied markets).

International Confex leads on meeting, with the tag line 'where the events industry meets' and the sub-title including 'a beacon of creativity, connection, and innovation for the events industry.'

IMEX Frankfurt highlights shared experience, saying 'building better human connections all over the world', with a subtitle of 'where the global meetings, events and incentive travel industry comes together for the largest trade show of its kind in Europe.'

IBTM Barcelona leads on the business angle, its differentiator, saying 'inspiring events for better business results.'

Each is carving out their slice of the market and applying strong brand visuals to differentiate their position.

How to reach your participants

Content marketing

Whatever multi-channel strategy you choose, content marketing will be central. Your Event Purpose Proposition, Story Pillars and Participant Personas all feed into this strategy, and your initial thinking will inform the content marketing strategy you create.

The goal is a seamless, omnichannel experience with consistent messaging. A helpful guideline is the 80/20 rule – 80% value-driven content, 20% promotion. Striking the right balance is crucial, as audiences resist hard sells.

Your content marketing can follow three core strategies, the first two of which are value-driven:

▶ **Event-led:** The bulk of your messaging – announcing speakers, brilliant panels, launching keynotes, the connection app, the board game evening. These posts provide value first, with a subtle call to action.

▶ **Content-led:** Broader industry insights, such as expert articles, market trends or legislative updates. Establishing credibility and positioning your event as a knowledge hub; many large events now publish industry newsletters.

▶ **Offer-led:** Focused on promotions – ticketing deadlines, limited-time discounts or tiered pricing. These messages create urgency and drive conversions (keep to under 20% of total).

The key is to tell great, engaging stories with a subtle call to action. The participant is the hero of your story and the focus of your gathering; stories that excite and engage will resonate. Avoid the 'we're delighted to announce our keynote speaker' – it's not about *your* excitement, it's about *their* wants.

Channels and strategies

Guide your team to build a multi-channel marketing strategy. While as a Chief Event Officer you won't be undertaking this task, you need to know what questions to ask. Your marketing strategy will be a mix of owned, paid, earned and organic media.

The website

Your website is the heart and soul of your marketing plan. Ensure the messaging, as well as the structure and usability is optimized for the customer experience.

Website forms – register your interest, download brochures or white papers, general enquiries – build a hot-list of engaged prospects – much like your past attendees and those contacted during event research.

Your data

Your own data is the obvious starting point: past delegates, members, subscribers. Analyse this against the size of your market to establish where the gaps are and how you fill them with external sources.

You may have a large database and a range of different messages you share with them; deciding the frequency and style of your event marketing, especially for an annual or flagship event, is vital. Too little – your message is lost. Too much, you lose the balance with the organizational comms.

Email

Email marketing is the foundation of a strong messaging strategy. Traditionally, it is the primary event promotion channel – used effectively it drives success. While your 'warm leads' (past delegates, members, VIPs) may respond well to emails, you'll also grow your list at the top of the funnel via inbound channels; advocacy, paid media and pay per click (PPC) can get the reach and engagement you may no longer be able to get from email.

Some worry about emailing 'too often'. Mass email blasts? No. But targeted segmented messaging, paired with the right offer and tone, delivers results.

Email thrives alongside strong lead generation. Once your event's tone is set, ensure consistent messaging across all communications for maximum impact.

PPC and paid media

PPC and paid media – ads on major platforms like LinkedIn, Meta and Google – vie with email for the biggest investment. LinkedIn ads are typically more expensive than other paid media, so work best supporting a high average customer value. Build a detailed

PPC and paid media programme – many outsource this specialist skill. Keep an eye on the trends; right now Google privileges content that meets the EEAT criteria – experience, expertise, authoritativeness and trust – but trends change.

Influencers
Advocacy marketing and word of mouth exist in every sector, and your Market Mapping process should ideally have sourced a list of the top dozen or so influencers. Building these social advocacy relationships can be time-consuming but remarkably effective, and such partnerships may include speaking at the event, how much coverage/how many posts they'll do.

Organic social media
Every market differs, but LinkedIn is key in most business markets – used organically, as well as through ads. You know your market sector. If Instagram and Facebook are channels of choice, explore a presence there, too. Whichever, leverage your tone of voice from your email marketing.

Socials are the place to showcase your content marketing stories, strong visuals and brand language, ideally with a touch of market-appropriate humour.

Media partnerships
Turning your Market Map media section into a cohesive list of potential marketing partners can help amplify your gathering and its importance in the marketplace.

Like influencers, this can be time-consuming to negotiate. Totally worth it. Especially if you're new to a market – demonstrates social proof – or in a competitive sector, where reach is invaluable.

Your media partnerships can also be checked against your original Market Map coverage and prioritized based on the sectors where you have less internal data.

The best marketing strategies for large events have dozens of marketing partnerships. Invest the time in doing this – it's about social proof as well as reach.

Delegate sales

Most effective with your warmest leads, or those who have already expressed an interest. Converting these leads or gaining any market insight from your sales team during the event lead time can be fed back into the process to iterate and improve.

SEO

Search engine optimization (SEO) is a purely organic tactic; ensure you have basic meta data on your website.

Funnels and loops

The sales or marketing funnel model is a helpful guide. You're selling tickets to your event, whether people pay for them or not. The marketing strategy takes customers through the process of awareness, consideration, desire and finally action – registration. When you build strong relationships with returning participants

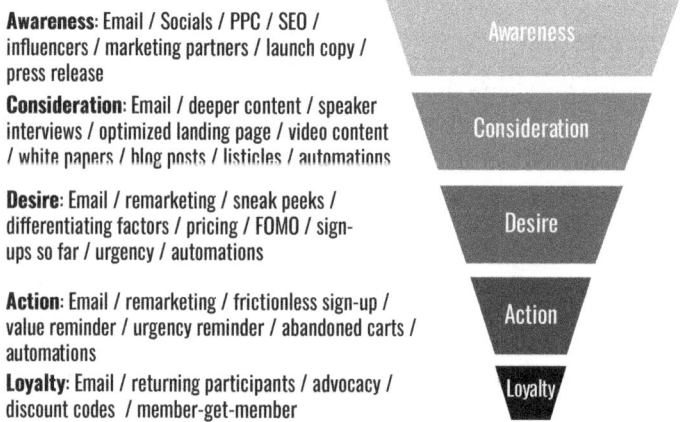

Event Marketing Funnel

Awareness: Email / Socials / PPC / SEO / influencers / marketing partners / launch copy / press release

Consideration: Email / deeper content / speaker interviews / optimized landing page / video content / white papers / blog posts / listicles / automations

Desire: Email / remarketing / sneak peeks / differentiating factors / pricing / FOMO / sign-ups so far / urgency / automations

Action: Email / remarketing / frictionless sign-up / value reminder / urgency reminder / abandoned carts / automations

Loyalty: Email / returning participants / advocacy / discount codes / member-get-member

Event marketing funnel

they might reach the loyalty and finally advocacy stages – where you encourage them to bring a colleague or share the message.

Think of your marketing channels through the lens of your funnel – at the top (TOFU) you've got PPC, SEO, socials, marketing partners and influencers who are bringing people to your website to sign up for more information. A small proportion may book directly, but you're more likely to need to lead–nurture those relationships to help them come to a purchasing decision.

Our Next Gen event goers are digital-first. And alternate models are serving them. The ACP funnel – audience, community, product – builds an audience, engages them with your community and *then* sells them your product (event).

Like the ACDA/AIDA (awareness, consideration, desire and action/awareness, interest, desire and action) funnel, the ACP funnel is linear. The rise of the Marketing Loop – an idea that conveys the continuous, iterative interactions between event owners (brands) and participants (consumers) – reflects a process where participants continuously re-engage with your event brand, at different stages of the traditional funnel, ultimately becoming brand advocates.

Marketing operations is vital to track your marketing strategy's results. Your team will need to decide on the tech stack, set up systems and integrations, optimize your CRM (if you have one) and how it connects to your marketing activity, build automations, analytics and reports. Event marketing consultant Helen Coetzee talked to me about data-driven attribution rather than a 'first touch' or 'last touch' approach; actively tracking your customer journey to understand the weighting of the various channels and activities that influence a booking.[7] Email might be the final conversation mechanism, but understanding the nuance helps you learn. This is a better approach than putting it all down to 'dark social' – untrackable.

Turning your media list into an effective partner programme

Marketing partnerships are a targeted way to reach your participants. Go back to your Stakeholder Map and explore both the media and influencers list – who can you negotiate a media partnership with? Will they help you promote the event? Will their logo on your website or socials give you additional status and social proof in the market?

Benchmark potential media and influencer partnerships against your own data to identify gaps and prioritize outreach. How much of your market have you already reached through existing relationships? Who can fill the gap? The goal: ensure your marketing plan covers every angle of a complex market.

Lead times

Event lead times – both production and marketing – are always a balancing act.

Production lead times: With the Event Purpose Proposition clear to the whole team, you can plan your event and any speakers or talent involved in the content well ahead – the bigger the profile, the longer the diary lead time. You'll horizon scan your sector to ensure that your date doesn't clash with major relevant events.

Marketing lead times: Promote your event with enough notice – the right lead time. This varies according to participant seniority, the sector and local business culture. Plus you need sufficient time to create the buzz and energy – to get your community excited and talking about the gathering. Lead times matter – consider it in relation to your event's scale.

Major events	3–5 years
Flagship annual event	2–3 years (for dates)
Large event	1 year–18 months
Smaller event	12–26 weeks

Shorter event horizons

The flip side of marketing lead times is audience behaviour. There seems to be a trend towards shorter event horizons; participants hesitant to commit too far in advance. There is less certainty for event marketers.

For a Hot Ticket event the audience may put it in the calendar and know they want to come months out. That doesn't necessarily mean they're buying a ticket straight away.

As an event marketing strategist your role is creating urgency, an element of FOMO (fear of missing out). Booking patterns have changed significantly in the last five years. Maritz's research shows that 45% delayed registration until four weeks prior, 22% until the final week and 9% book onsite.[8] These figures vary based on industry; but can be nail-biting for you and your team – the challenge is to find the right levers in your world to encourage and excite your audiences.

These levers may be around discount pricing models, extra benefits for early registrations (private meetings with celebrities, partner giveaway gifts) and creating the momentum that the whole community will be there. Can you afford to miss out?

Pricing can influence near-term participant behaviour; trends are moving away from 'early bird' models, and more sophisticated tiered pricing models are now common.

Learn from consumer brands

Business events are a mature market – dynamic yet still evolving – and they are learning from consumer brands and bringing those insights to the participant experience. Concepts like the Marketing Loop discussed above help Chief Event Officers stay fresh in their approach.

Registrations is another great example. Your team has done so much strategic and tactical work to get your potential attendee to the booking form. You want to make it super easy for them to sign on the digital dotted line.

If your event registration asks multiple questions – interests, job level, sub-sector drop-downs and offers more than five pricing options – you're very likely to lose me.

Get this information post-registration. At the registration moment, the focus is closing the sale.

Consumer brands have mastered frictionless purchasing – thanks to Shopify and purchase psychology. Likewise, an intuitive event registration system can both boost bookings and enhance user experience. Simplify your event signup and optimize your tech stack.

Monitoring your abandoned cart rate is a simple way to measure registration simplicity. This hovers around 70% for retail purchases in the UK. Abandoned cart automations – a gentle reminder email – can reduce these rates. Also an opportunity to connect personally, leveraging your tone of voice; who doesn't love an email titled '[First], your cart is calling to you – here's a discount code.'

Reaching sponsors and exhibitors

Sponsor storytelling

Your potential partners, sponsors and exhibitors need their own stories, too. Targeted messaging promoting the value of engaging with your gathering.

Taking the 'sell' side of your Stakeholder Map, work through a similar process for your partners. How much data do you have? Who can you partner with to fill the gaps in your market? How do you research your sales targets?

You may have lengthy existing relationships or you may be starting afresh – either way you'll need to establish the partnership benefits and what stories you're telling to whom.

Are sponsors looking for lead generation? Do they want to align themselves with your big idea? Are they launching a new product? Are they crucial to the sector supply-chain and just need to be there?

Create sales messages – website / proposals – that meet their needs, offer social proof from previous sponsors, easy visual ways to understand the 'shape' of the whole event, its differentiators, testimonials. Your initial partner marketing should encourage inbound response and understanding their potential investment level. You want pre-qualified leads in your funnel.

Consider when in the sales cycle you share package pricing. Leveraging your tech-stack to automate the outreach/in reach process saves time, but the important work is building a depth of understanding of your target market, their needs and wants. You may want to build out Partner/Sponsor personas, understanding their motivations and the appropriate messages.

Consultative vs commodity sales approach

Selling exhibition space is often a transactional or commodity-based approach; typically based on higher volume sales, lower customer interaction and lower price. If you're selling back-of-the-room exhibition tables at a confex, or smaller stands on square metreage at a trade show or expo, this is the ideal approach.

Here, the price is transparent, although you may offer upsell add-ons to the package, but it can be very light touch from a salesperson perspective.

Consultative sales are underpinned by relationships, understanding the potential partners' dreams and desires and creating an often bespoke package that delivers value. Assign your most sophisticated salespeople to creating and negotiating these packages.

Your client may be looking for a brand activation to encourage people to engage directly with their organizations – think Netflix's *Squid Game* activation at Advertising Week Europe, or The Meet in MinneSODA Lounge from Meet Minneapolis at the

Professional Convention Management Association event, replete with the sale team dressed as soda bar staff and a drinks menu including Visionary Fizz, Global Summit, The Innovator and The Networker.

If the client is seeking more relationships, you might build bespoke micro-events into their package – VIP dinners and breakfasts, targeted at specific groups, or if they want serious visibility you might explore a high-level speaker, while ensuring that the content is not sales-driven. Show, don't tell. Have a clear strategy for 'pay for play' speaker slots: what types of speakers? How much editorial control? Do you allow them at all?

Building long-term partnerships

These relationship-driven partnerships can form the bedrock of multi-year relationships. Imagine if married couples got divorced each year and then sought a new partner for the next year.

Event partnerships are evolving, and the most powerful conversations are longer term, with your partners working in lockstep with you, as your gatherings help deliver ongoing value. This approach also secures both revenue and event longevity; taking a longer-term view is good for everyone.

Long-term partnerships are about deep listening. Get under the skin of your sponsors' and partners' needs, the strategic direction of their business and how you can support them in achieving their aims.

Third-party events

Of course, for corporates, not all events are owned, and you may engage with third-party events as sponsors or exhibitors. But the messaging and marketing strategies are the same: work through the Event Purpose Proposition and create a bespoke marketing strategy, with your Market Map and messaging plan to ensure you reach your intended goals.

Sponsor activations at large trade shows are event projects in their own right. A huge creative process goes into developing the stories and branding; ensure that your messaging plan reaches your target market, working in partnership with the show owner, as well as using your own channels.

Crucially, you'll want to find good, motivating reasons for people to come by your stand. Meet us at Stand GL235 is not an enticing message – do you have prize draws? A quiz? Great food? An on-stand band?

Building VIP relationships

Just as the Japanese *nemawashi* process informally builds support before a decision, the same applies to event audiences. By the time your event is public, your VIP groundwork should already be in place.

Start with a VIP wish list – at all levels of your organization. I recommend doing this at the Market Map Stage, identifying the 'must-have' attendees who will drive the right conversations. Do you need a core group of top Procurement Directors? Build a hyper-targeted list, send personalized invitations and maybe host an exclusive Procurement Directors' Club. Or is it about landing that elusive senior health executive, non-governmental organization leader, or policymaker?

Your board likely has key relationships – even if they're distanced from the event itself. Getting senior buy-in early can be game-changing. As one CMO told me, 'You need the board to call their contacts. Some even attend – they're a draw in themselves.'

Develop a VIP strategy and socialize it across the teams. Encourage personal outreach – emails, WhatsApps, VIP codes – whatever it takes to get the right people in the room.

Press, media and the comms community

Unless your event is under Chatham House Rules (and even then you can share the conversation, just not the speaker), a media presence can be a major contributor to telling the story before, at and after the event. Major media coverage demonstrates impact.

When I launched the Virtual Worlds Forum in 2007, we were a tiny organization, but I hired a brilliant old-school PR professional. The launch event received coverage in *The Times*, *The Guardian*, BBC News, Reuters and all the major blogs and influencers of the time. This coverage amplified the first-year event – having a major impact on speaker recruitment and sponsorship sales for the following year.

Building your comms strategy

Your comms team or PR partner will ideally take the ideas in your Messaging Grid, the programme content and the speakers and talent and their ideas, and run this through the filter of your Event Purpose Proposition and your organization's communication strategy.

Is the event about signing up campaign signatories, like the Tech Talent Charter? Is the purpose to launch your comms strategy? Does your event have multiple messaging strands that link to the corporate or organizational purpose? If so, in the weeks prior to the event, you'll want to clarify these and start inviting press and social influencers.

Establish what outcomes you're aiming for. Is this about audience reach, socials, press mentions? Or are you looking for your CEO or key speakers to get interviewed by the press? Or are you launching comms stories that have clear follow-up?

Translating your event messaging into a clear comms strategy helps you create a sophisticated media plan to ensure the right interviews and media activity for key speakers, sponsors and partners.

On-the-day film and photography

Gatherings are moments in time – without video, photos, media and user-generated content, little remains.

Strong event-day creative content starts with strategy. Ask: what stories do we want to tell afterward? The vast community? Deals made? Groundbreaking ideas?

Give photographers and videographers a clear brief detailing must-have images for live, post-event and next year's marketing. Prioritize real-time social content with rapid turnaround and direct sharing to the social team.

Work closely with comms to align video outputs and messaging. Schedule key interviews in advance – CEOs and government officials won't do impromptu vox pops without prior coordination.

On the day: speed and agility are everything.

Delivering powerful long-term outcomes

Transformative events live on in the conversations and the long-tail assets the Chief Event Officer has created.

Working closely with your policy or public affairs team can make all the difference.

Eszter Mattiassich-Aszody, Head of Global Events at Siemens Healthineers, shared a game-changing example from her time at Siemens AG. Her team was tasked with booking a marquee and catering for a windfarm opening in South Australia – deep in the outback, three hours from Adelaide. Key government and press stakeholders were unlikely to attend due to the distance.

Collaborating with Government Affairs, they reframed the event. The windfarm, built on an Aboriginal site, aligned with Indigenous traditions and national net-zero goals. The idea: unveil an Aboriginal painting on the turbine, merging renewable energy with cultural storytelling and creating a community-driven event with local schools and farmers.

The result? A chartered flight from Canberra, high-profile government and media attendance, and widespread praise. Ministers celebrated community unity, while Siemens gained invaluable press coverage and a reputational boost.

Images last forever. Award-winning event photographer Paul Clarke expertly captures speakers at their most engaging. He warns that speaking to slides looks wooden in photos, and bored panellists are forever recorded. His advice: 'Look up, meet the audience, smile and engage – the event lives on in media.'

Memorable outcomes don't happen by accident.

Author and activist Caroline Criado-Perez, author of the *Sunday Times* best-seller *Invisible Women: Exposing Data Bias in a World Designed for Men* and creator of the concept of the 'gender data gap', keynoted the Open Data Institute's Summit in 2019, which asked the big question 'how can we improve the impact of data?' Her campaigning work includes getting a female historical figure on Bank of England banknotes; getting Twitter to introduce a 'report abuse' button on tweets and getting the first statue of a woman – suffragette Millicent Fawcett – in London's Parliament Square.

I knew when I made a speaker badge for Poppy, her pet dog, and asked to put it on Poppy's collar, that the photo on socials would break the internet and help shine a light on the conversation that day.

Preparing for the gathering

Atul Gawande's book *The Checklist Manifesto* leverages his experience as a surgeon and the challenges of modern medicine and merges this with experience from complex property building and airline pilots, to explore how professionals deal with the increasing complexity of their responsibilities.

The Chief Event Officer's Playbook has worked through the 'why are you creating this event' questions and the 'who is this event for' questions.

The next stage is to understand how you create, curate and craft the event experience. What actually happens on the day?

PART 3
WHAT WILL THE EVENT EXPERIENCE BE?

Chapter 6
Curating the content

Content is the heart and soul of business events. When asked 'what makes a good attendee experience?' the AMEX GBT 2025 Global Forecast found that event content and agenda was the highest response, topping the list at 38%.[1]

Content, in whatever form, is central to nearly all business events. The conversations, the presentations, the panels, the stories, the talent, the stilt walker with a bubble machine, the speakers, these are the core elements that differentiate business and professional events from the myriad other events in the industry.

Weddings, festivals, parties and sports events are all powerful gatherings, but business events' magic is the promise that you will learn something, experience something, be changed in some way. Whether you leave with your mind blown by the latest developments in quantum computing or inspired by a coffee-queue conversation about how AI is changing surgery, the moments you curate, the events you create are about sharing ideas, increasing knowledge, taking inspiration back to the office (or coffee shop).

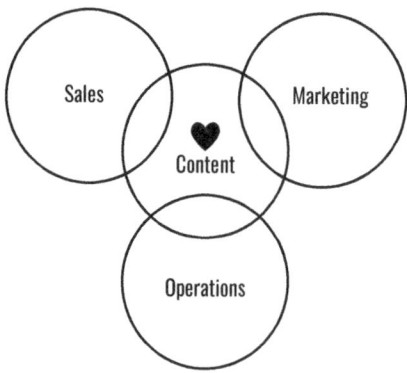

Content at the heart of the process

People convene *around* the content. While the connections, community and celebrations that happen around business events can be seen as the glue that holds people together, the content elements are the building blocks of the gathering.

How to get this right is the third big question in the *Playbook* – 'what will the event experience be?'

We've explored the two big opening questions – why are you doing this event, and who is it for? Within that we've understood the ideas of transformation, journey and purpose and how to map your stakeholders and amplify the message of the event.

With these questions resolved, you can look deeper into 'what' the actual event experience will be.

We'll be exploring these with three questions:

- ▶ How will you curate the content?
- ▶ How will you craft the experience?
- ▶ How will you reimagine the welcome?

Let's start with the content.

And the content starts with knowing what you want it to do.

What world do you want your event to create?

When you create a gathering, you create a world. Your attendees step into that world. A temporary, immersive world.

Done well, it's a fabulous hybrid of theatre, intellectual debate, immersive storytelling, a brilliant dinner party and a community fete. We want our events to be welcoming, induce curiosity, inspire participants to do something different when they get back to their desk/laptop and create long-lasting connections.

When you get it right, your attendees are deeply immersed and enmeshed in the world you created, having the experiences you designed. Absorbing the vibe. Meeting the people. Having those great aha! moments.

Adam Parry, founder of Event Tech Live and Event Industry News, recalls a game-changing event: one of the first Web Summits in Dublin.

Two things struck him – event design and technology. The Web Summit team didn't just focus on the conference; they curated the Night Summit and Surf Summit, seamlessly blending business and leisure. 'All that wraparound stuff was great – I didn't have to figure out my evenings. It was the first event I attended that truly mixed work and play.' Strategic brand-hosted parties – think Facebook, Xerox – funnelled attendees back into the main event.

Then, there was the tech. 'They were way ahead on matchmaking,' Adam says. 'For the first time, I could pre-scan attendees and schedule meetings. It was a real turning point.'

He arrived knowing no one. By the time he left, he'd made a mountain of connections. Web Summit didn't just host an event – it engineered networking at scale.

Those serendipitous meetings are powerful, shaping the sense of wonder and delight. And when that serendipity is purposefully designed, even more powerful.

Your events are communities of transformative experiences. Your events can change the world.

So don't forget, Chief Event Officers, you're a world maker.

I invite you to consider what world you want your event to create. Do you want it to be welcoming? Curiosity inducing? Inspirational? Immersive? Campaign-led? Story-led? The choice is yours.

Bringing your organization's story to life

When you host an event your participants – delegates, sponsors, exhibitors, VIPs, speakers, media – experience your brand brought to life.

Whatever your organization's values, when your participants walk through the door of your event they are immersed in you and what you do. Your brand, or your organization, manifested into being. It's crucial to do this authentically and accurately, to push the creative boundaries while working within the framework of your brief.

For example, New Scientist Live calls itself 'the world's greatest festival of ideas and discoveries – everything you love about science, technology and the wonders of our world'.[2]

New Scientist Live brings *New Scientist* magazine to life.[3] The multiplatform brand delivers products across print, digital and live events for the science-curious including: the subscription magazine, online magazine, The New Scientist Academy with online courses to help you 'feed your fascination for science', Discovery Tours, branded items and a jobs board.

New Scientist Live brings all that together – it's a mind-blowing festival of ideas and discoveries, with opportunities to explore the frontiers of science while engaging with the brand and its brand extensions.

Or *Stylist* magazine, a free print fashion and lifestyle magazine targeted at affluent 20–40-year-old female commuters, with content around fashion, travel, beauty, people and careers.[4] There's also an online magazine, an app, Strong Women run clubs and VIP member events.

Stylist Live is the flagship event – three days, thousands of women, 14 live catwalk shows, curated marketplace with 100+ brands, multiple stages, some of the finest food and drink to elevate the experience and the 'the most uplifting, joyful atmosphere' all under one roof.

Both of these events bring the unique energy of their respective brands, creating experiences and activations that are engaging and immersive, solidifying the relationships participants have with the brand and ultimately the people they meet.

For media brands, it can feel quite easy to just add Live! to the brand – but it does what it says on the tin. Your event is your community's, or members', or customers' chance to experience everything about your organization. To feel the quality. To deeply understand your values, how you live then and how you bring them to life.

Is it the cheapest stand build you've ever seen with minimal branding and packed to the rafters? That says 'we're all about the money' not 'we're all about your experience'.

Is there a red carpet as you walk up to the exhibition centre? A jazz trio welcoming participants? Or close-up magicians or acrobats entertaining people while they queue? Is the badge tech super-slick and you've over-staffed the Welcome Area with your smiling team supporting everyone? That says 'we care about your experience, and we want you to have the best time'.

While larger events clearly need huge staff teams with much of the operational side outsourced, having your team onsite and talking to participants is your best brand promotion. And your team get to do non-stop market research; understanding your clients, community or members, their values, their style, their questions.

The first step in content design is underpinned with this one idea. You're not just putting on an event. You're welcoming your community to step inside your organization and experience you in a deep and meaningful way.

Genuinely curated content

Everyone's a content creator in our social media age.

The volume of content can be overwhelming. As a professional you need to keep up. There can actually be a degree of shame when you *haven't* read that obscure latest research. You want to read professional journals and articles. You have favourite websites for news updates and content, multiple social channels. You may be in a Slack/Discord/WhatsApp channel or 10 where people share information. You may look at LinkedIn or other professional network platforms in your field every day, or week, or month. Or hour.

The information bombarding you is somewhere on the overpowering to unmanageable continuum.

The power of events is that the content is curated.

Someone, hopefully astute and thoughtful, has trawled through all that. They've researched the key drivers and big ideas with dozens of people, found the interesting nuggets, latest startups, newest ideas and future trends.

They understand your market's needs: how much listening do they want to do? How much talking and sharing with peers? What's the balance of panels and firesides to presentations? This will be different in every sector. They've unearthed those brand-new-to-the-market ideas, evaluated the call for speakers and synthesized all of that into an attention-grabbing must-attend event.

If your participants trust your brand – and they should – then one of the inherent attendee drivers is that they trust *you* to curate the best content. They want to spend one/two/three days at your event and soak up the brightest, best, most left-field fascinating ideas and inspiration and take that back to their workplace. While, of course, connecting, talking and exploring.

They want to leave inspired, and the way you structure the content is key. The content is more than curation; it's a reflection of your brand and its values.

Leigh Gilmore is Global Head of Live Experiences at Bloomberg, leading the creation of experiences that extend Bloomberg Media's editorial vision, amplifying the brand, unlocking revenue and cultivating communities.

Bloomberg is one of the biggest media partners at the World Economic Forum at Davos. In 2024, Leigh launched Bloomberg House – just steps away from the Forum's Congress Centre, with a packed schedule of programming.

Leigh combines a depth of storytelling with inspiring content, infused with a sense of strong brand marketing. Bloomberg House is the real content deal.

Leigh told me:

> *Bloomberg House is all about substance…*
>
> *My goal is always to ensure the event goes beyond a single moment… to tell a compelling narrative. When guests walk through the doors of Bloomberg House, they're not just entering an event – they're stepping into a living, breathing representation of the Bloomberg brand…. Every detail… is meticulously curated to reflect our brand values.*
>
> *… The real opportunity is in fostering an emotional connection between our guests and the brand. You want them to experience Bloomberg in a way that's personal and memorable – so much so that they… feel compelled to share it. The ultimate goal is for each guest to become an advocate for our brand in the wider world.[5]*

What is the content?

It's nearly 30 years since Bill Gates wrote his 'content is king' essay.

Much of his argument – that content will be a revenue driver for the internet, as it was with broadcasting, that online content needs depth, interactivity and personal involvement compared the 'letters to the editor' page and that the 'internet' will be a marketplace of ideas, experiences and products – is equally true of live events.

Great, engaging content lies at the heart of most successful events. Content really is king. Whether that's a rockstar speaker in your field, or a rockstar with something profound to say about your field, or a perambulatory theatrical production that explores the core ideas of your agenda, or a poet opening your event with a poem about data, content is the driving force that communicates the ideas you want people to explore.

Indeed, at its very simplest, whether your organization has a commercial imperative or is a non-profit, your event is a marketplace of ideas, experiences and products.

It doesn't matter whether you're:

- ▶ A corporate convening your global leaders to agree the five-year strategy

- ▶ A media owner hosting a conference around its major media property's conversations

- ▶ An association bringing together your members to create new policy directions

- ▶ A commercial conference or trade-show organizer genuinely creating a market – convening all the players

- ▶ A government department hosting an event for a specific market sector

For each of these, the content is at the heart of the gathering. Eleanor Roosevelt is often quoted saying 'great minds discuss ideas; average minds discuss events; small minds discuss people.'

Ideas are the core of events; the great minds at our gatherings are energized by insightful ideas, presented in compelling ways by a diverse group of people: thinkers, creators, industry specialists and luminaries.

When Deloitte, the largest professional services organization in the world, hosted its 2024 US Partner, Principal and Managing Director Meeting at Vegas Sphere for 8,000 colleagues it was the Women and Allies panel with Olympic gymnastics medallist Simone Biles, tennis legend Billie Jean King and US basketball coach Dawn Staley that made the news. The content, the talent, the conversation is a big slice of what counts.

But be strategic. A big sports personality with a great story to tell is not enough. What all of these events share is a need to convene your community *around* the content.

One significant way to do this is to create your content around One Central Idea, question or provocation.

One big question?

You might decide to articulate one big question. The Open Data Institute (ODI) – an institute founded by Sir Tim Berners-Lee and Sir Nigel Shadbolt – is especially good at this, with summits themed around a specific provocation.

The ODI helps organizations build trust in data, uniting businesses, governments and civil society to tackle real-world challenges.

In late 2020, six months into the Covid pandemic, its in-person summit was reimagined as a digital event. Data had shifted from a niche topic to a daily fixture in news broadcasts, political briefings and health trackers. The ODI team posed a pressing question: 'How Can Humanity Harness the Power of Data in a Changing

World?' At a time of global upheaval, when data was critical to understanding the virus and shaping responses, this was more relevant than ever.

By 2021, the conversation had evolved beyond data itself to its human impact. The theme shifted to 'What Does It Mean to Be Human in a World of Data?'

A strong provocation drives meaningful discussions – framing keynotes, panels and debates that challenge participants to explore, reflect and rethink their sector's future. The question must be broad enough to sustain engagement yet focused enough to remain impactful. Get it right, and it shapes the entire event's success.

Media agency PHD UK's event 'Is Optimism Dead?' explored the power of optimism through fresh research and expert insights. PHD leveraged the event to unveil new findings on British consumer sentiment on optimism and analysed its implications for brands. The event featured lively discussions: journalists Kevin Maguire and Sam Lister debated optimism in politics and the economy; author Amy Kean examined collective voices' potential; Omnicon's Phil Rowley explored tech's role in shaping optimism; and author and tech founder Bruce Daisley reflected on the future of work. The event demonstrated how anchoring content around a compelling question can drive engagement and deliver actionable insights.

What's your theme?

'What's the conference theme?' is a common question from speakers, partners and participants. A well-crafted theme is more than a tagline – it's a powerful platform communicating your event's purpose in a short-attention world and a good alternative to the big question provocation.

I've sat through countless Content Committee and Advisory Board meetings where 'eureka' moments result in vague themes like The Way Forward or Celebrating Success. But a theme isn't a title – it needs to unify your event's core ideas.

Finding the right theme is an art: broad enough to be inclusive, yet specific enough to add meaning. It should serve as the totem pole for your content – sometimes for an entire year.

There's at least one event which has had the theme 'How do we get the next 10 years right?' for 10 years.

That's not a theme. While it's a good question, and could be a good question each year, it's also a moveable feast of a title that you can hang pretty much any topic of conversation or presentation on.

A good theme requires specificity. To establish your theme, explore your market sector drivers. This is an ongoing conversation; in an ideal world you will have your theme or provocation at launch. People need an idea to engage with, to start their internal conversation about involvement.

IBTM World – Incentives, Business Travel and Meetings – hosts its global event for the MICE sector (meetings, incentives, conferences and events industry) in Barcelona each year, convening over 15,000 participants.

The broad theme 'Inspiring Events for Better Business Results' gives you a taster of what you might expect; inspiration (for you), as well as ideas about inspirational events, all focused on delivering better business results. Given that it's a trade show, owned by RX, there's also an express business development purpose: 'engineered to give you a year's worth of profitable leads in just three days.'[6]

When you gather your senior stakeholders to talk about the triumvirate of Transformation, Journey and Purpose that should surface conversation around the big ideas and drivers. What are the major trends in your field? Impact of AI? Sustainability? Diversity?

The Global Fashion Summit, held in Copenhagen in June 2025, had the theme 'Bridging barriers in sustainable fashion'. *Vogue* magazine's PhotoVogue Festival – the conscious fashion photography festival, bridging ethics and aesthetics – had the theme 'The Tree of Life: A Love Letter to Nature' for its 2025 Milan edition. The World Economic Forum, held in Davos, Switzerland each January, had the 2024 theme 'Rebuilding trust' and the 2025 theme 'Collaborating for the intelligent age'.

For your event to have the desired impact, you'll need to develop, test and iterate your theme or question, headline or title until you're sure it absolutely resonates with your market. Talk to past participants, speakers and advisors.

Hard content and soft content

I differentiate between hard and soft content; when developing content, you need to establish which is the priority upfront.

Hard content – is ideas first. Designed so it's both attention-grabbing and thoughtful. You'll brief your speakers really well – more of that later. Hard content is about speaker-led learning and exploring.

Soft content – is people first, and your ability to create environments where people can connect around ideas. You create places and spaces for participants to meet and share, but the content of their conversations is only loosely pre-defined.

Soft social – is people and connection. I do not love the word networking; I believe that 'the networking drinks' have had their day. While they work for some, I prefer to think of them as 'connection gatherings' – opportunities for people to meet others on a human level.

Which to privilege?

Whether you design the soft content first – informal spaces for relaxation and collaboration, social events or opportunities for both planned and serendipitous connections – or the hard content – the shape of the day, big speakers, annual general meeting (AGM) requirements – depends on your priorities.

Content strategy

Whenever I speak at events, I ask participants the same question: 'Would you rather hear the biggest-name speaker in your field or sit at a table with 10 peers, sharing insights?'

Post-pandemic, most choose peer discussions. This trend started in the late 2010s, with event designs fostering conversation, but now it's accelerating – over 70% prefer roundtables over rockstars.

What does this mean for content? You still need headline speakers as a draw, especially for attendees navigating approval processes. But the real magic lies in balancing marquee names with interactive, personal discussions – where big ideas meet real engagement.

Hard content
While not an exhaustive list, this gives you some ideas of the type of formats you might explore.

- Keynotes and presentations – limit to 30 minutes (ideally 20 in our TikTok world) and ensure speakers are saying something they've not said elsewhere. And with a lot of well-moderated Q&A. Be nervous of speakers who won't take questions.

- Fireside chats and 'in conversations' – speakers and participants increasingly want this; speakers need less presentation, participants find it more engaging and a good sparring partner can unearth untold gold.

- Panels – not more than four people. Curated to explore opposing views, with a well-briefed moderator and pre-briefing call to explore headline issues.

- Workshops and roundtables – participants want to shared lived experience and hear from others.

- High speed formats
  - Lightning talks – short, sharp 3–5-minute fast-paced, high-impact presentations, speakers deliver concise, compelling insights, cutting straight to the core of an idea
  - Pechakucha or Ignite talks – a high-energy format, speakers showcase 20 slides, each auto-advancing every 20 seconds (Pechakucha) or 15 seconds (Ignite). Both force sharp, visually driven narrative that keeps audiences engaged

▷ Breaking the fourth wall[7] formats
- O Fishbowls – participatory format; a small group debates a topic in an inner circle while a larger audience observes. Works best in the round; participants rotate in and out to keep the conversation fresh
- O Hackathons – tech-born marathon for rapid prototyping and high-speed creative innovation
- O Campfires – informal and interactive sessions, encouraging participation
- O Unconferences – from the 1980s tech world, with Tim O'Reilly an early pioneer. User-generated content writ-large and live – the participants create the agenda when the gathering begins

Unconferences can give participants a sense of ownership and deep engagement. WPP's Stream conference calls itself the '(un) conference for (un)conventional thinkers'. Named by Wired as one of the world's best tech conferences, it's an invite-only gathering for marketing, media and tech leaders, hosted by global creative agency WPP.

Unlike traditional conferences, Stream thrives on interactive, provocative debate under Chatham House Rules, with an organic agenda. Past participants include Sheryl Sandberg, Nassim Taleb, Daniel Ek, Nicola Mendelsohn, Jeffrey Katzenberg and Gwyneth Paltrow, alongside top brand leaders, tech giants, venture capitalists (VCs), founders, artists, filmmakers, academics and economists.

One attendee said to me, 'It's got a very charming, outdoorsy feel, with deep discussions. It's quite the hot ticket.'

Laurent Ezekiel, CMO at WPP told me, 'The creative power of the participant-led conversation is that ideas are born and innovation happens.'[8]

Participant experience trumps taxonomy and not all content fits into neat categories – new formats emerge constantly, often sparking attendee imagination.

The International Congress of Parkinson's Disease and Movement Disorders unites 5,000 experts annually to share research and best practices. Hosted by The Movement Disorders Society (MDS), it fosters collaboration among clinicians, researchers and industry leaders.

A standout is the Video Challenge, a lively, humour-infused session where top experts analyse ethics-approved movement disorder videos, debating diagnoses prior to the revelation of the actual diagnosis. This engaging, science-driven event brings a light touch to a challenging field, blending serious learning with a relaxed, memorable experience.

Soft content

Soft content is people-centric, helping them convene around an idea, without forcing the conversation.

▶ Themed tables – whether poseur tables or lunch tables, with clear themes for people to gravitate towards: sustainability, workforce, AI, diversity, possibly colour-coded to match the programme guide

▶ Cosy corners – chill sofa areas designed to encourage people to connect and share, can likewise be themed

▶ Birds of a feather sessions – started in the tech sector in the 1960s; informal gatherings of people around a specific topic, with an unplanned agenda

▶ Live polling – a great way to both ask the audience and track the sentiment of the room – also helps foster conversation

▶ World Café – an informal, structured discussion; participants rotate between small group conversations, fostering collaborative dialogue, knowledge sharing and idea generation in a relaxed, café-style setting

▶ Badge Question Box – great for smaller events, a large box on the badge left blank for participants to write 'what

I'm looking for', 'what I'd like to learn today' – or your core gathering question. Great for sparking conversation, especially in sub-150 people events

▶ Lanyard colours – colour coding your different categories of attendees – startups, VCs, academics – to help them easily find each other

▶ Connection or networking
   O Drinks – you either love or hate the networking drinks. Tips: walk purposefully through the room. Approach someone standing alone; most people are kind. Ask questions. Know how to leave: 'Great meeting you, enjoy the rest of the evening.'
   O Structured networking – all eliminate the awkwardness of aimless networking
      – Speed-dating – a series of short, timed meetings; participants efficiently exchanging ideas and contacts. Exhausting for some
      – Braindates – automated networking while preserving personal connection, facilitating knowledge sharing. Participants post questions or topics, then connect for 1:1 or group discussions
      – Tech-enabled short double opt-in meetings ensure mutual interest and connection maximization
   O Small group activities – local tours, board game nights, whatever resonates with your participants – make for easier connections. With an increasingly deeper understanding of participant diversity – neurodiversity, introverts, extroverts and those who thrive (or don't) in large social settings, event design is always evolving.

Soft social and networking

Participants most want connections and networking. Our role as Chief Event Officers is to enable it, effortlessly. From the 'turn to your neighbour and introduce yourself' in the welcome speech to lots of easy places to chill and connect.

At many events, hardcore delegates enjoy the coffee lounge all day; I remember one delegate efficiently having 'the first coffee of the day' every 40 minutes with a different lead.

We talk about serendipity – and those genuinely serendipitous moments are uplifting. Curated serendipity – combining deliberate experience design with the unexpected delight of chance encounters – takes it to the next level. Stop hoping, start hosting. Networking makes many people anxious so design for a meaningful connection. Maybe it's time to appoint a Head of Serendipity.

The Future Proof Festival (our 5C example in the Introduction) hosts the Breakthru Meeting Programme. Meetings are transparently designed to spark meaningful connections with decision-makers, build partnerships, boost ROI and achieve business objectives. Attendees can join up to 24 double opt-in meetings – both people agree to meet each other – held at tables across an acre of dedicated meeting space.

Shoptalk, at the intersection of retail, technology and innovation, was co-founded in 2015 by Anil Aggarwal, Jonathan Weiner and Simran Rekhi Aggarwal and acquired in 2019 by Hyve Group, plc. In addition to the Hosted Programme, Shoptalk Spring 2025 hosted Meetup, delivering 75,000 double opt-in 15-minute onsite meetings (from 375,000 requests).

Contemporary event design aims to bring the intimacy, immediacy and purpose of 1:1 meetings to events of scale. Leveraging technology to do this gives participants the intentional connection outcome without the pain of having to find the right people.

At the heart of the content and experiences you curate is listening to your audience. Here's an event that created a soft social activity that absolutely delivered.

The 2025 Caravan Camping & Motorhome Show at Birmingham's NEC isn't just a trade event – it's a 95,000-strong pilgrimage for the UK's caravan and motorhome faithful. Organized by the National Caravan Council (NCC), a trade association, the show pulls together the entire supply chain: manufacturers, holiday and residential parks, dealerships, suppliers and service providers.

The NCC are experts at listening to their audience. Strategically timed for half-term, it's the ultimate family day out, complete with high-stakes pester power – 'Mum, Dad, THIS one!' – as kids pick their dream camper.

Smack in the middle of the hall? A lake. Little adventurers can kayak and try SUP (stand-up paddleboarding), while parents observe from dryland at the Watersports Café. Nearby, the Beach Café comes with a helter-skelter and picnic area.

The lake might be at the centre of the show, but the customer is at the heart of the experience: happy kids = happy parents = happy buyers. Everything else is commentary.

How do you research the content

The magic of business gatherings lies in their immediacy – content that's fresh, relevant and thought-provoking. It's not a journal article that spent months in review – great event content captures the now.

What sets a successful event apart is the quality of pre-event listening. Have you truly heard your audience? Your partners?

Steve Jobs famously dismissed conventional market research, saying, 'People don't know what they want until you show it to them.' The challenge of innovative content is to take what you hear and think several steps ahead. Have you crafted something they don't yet know they need?

British author Alan Moore, primarily known for his graphic novels including *V for Vendetta* and *Watchmen*, put it even more succinctly: 'It's not the job of the artist to give the audience what they want. If the audience knew what they needed, they wouldn't be the audience. They would be the artists.' Great content doesn't just reflect demand – it shapes it.

Joe Pine told me 'people want to go beyond merely memorable to those truly transformative experiences. Transformations have aspirants – not attendees – if you understand your participants aspirations, what they're missing in their life or business, you can design an event to help them make that great leap.'[9]

Listening and insight fuel strong content development. While attendee feedback – via surveys, interviews and social listening – is crucial, true innovation comes from synthesizing that data into meaningful insights. You need to understand your audience's personas, their challenges and what keeps them up at night.

Take a cue from *The Times*, *Sunday Times* and Times Radio, who invite readers to join research panels – occasional short surveys that help them fine-tune the content they deliver.

While an overarching content vision is key, programming doesn't need to be locked in at once. A phased approach is helpful for both talent recruitment and marketing – secure keynotes and high-profile speakers early, then complete with diverse voices. Always leave space for last-minute hot topics – that final, finger-on-the-pulse slot ensures your event stays relevant.

Market research strategies

There are three stages to developing a content strategy and the content you deliver within it:

- ▶ Understanding the market and its drivers
- ▶ Exploring all available content from all angles
- ▶ Curating the best content into an energizing programme

In complex and mature markets, the lead content programmer may well have a strong sense of the market, its drivers and the latest trends. However, everyone has inherent bias – 'favourite speakers' and networks you're already engaged in.

Creating and curating content is somewhere an art and a science; leveraging the best of marketing research skills to ensure a full understanding of your attendees wants and needs. Talking direct to your market is one of the most powerful ways to understand their concerns and build a programme that meets their needs.

There's a number of ways to do this:

▶ Qualitative research

▶ Surveys

▶ Social channel research

▶ Feedback analysis from previous events

Qualitative research calls deliver value and can be synthesized into a new understanding of market needs.

For both research and surveys, consider referencing the people you reach against your Persona Messaging Grid and Market Map. Your research needs to reflect all the areas of your market. With a repeat or regular event, find ways to survey or speak to people who *don't* attend; otherwise your research and ultimately thinking is referencing the same people repeatedly.

There are very few event market sectors that aren't mature, complex and with multiple competitors, so ensuring your research reaches every corner of your market will ultimately help you deliver an event that has attendees saying 'whoah, how did they *know* what I'm thinking?'. One way to achieve that is to ensure that your market research has a high percentage of new people/non-attendees, perhaps 15–20%.

Call for papers

Many scientific and clinical events traditionally relied on the Call for Papers model. Its use is growing in commercial events, driven by advancing technology.

The advantage is speed, the downside is volume and there's no quality guarantee. The higher profile your event the larger the number of speaking applications. SXSW London 2025 had 2,500 applications for 500 slots in its launch show. The Content Lead for a sector trade show, programming a two-stream two-day event, received over 160 applications, so around a 2:1 ratio.

While it can feel advantageous to have a deadline and cut-off point, and you may have applications from people and topics you may not have considered, calls for papers are best used in conjunction with a robust research methodology.

How do you create cadence and flow?

Great content programming is like a well-composed symphony, balancing highs and lows, interaction and reflection, content and connection.

The narrative arc of your event content – the journey – should ideally hook participants upfront, create curiosity and help them feel invested, ending with a sense of transformation and celebration. Create both peak and memorable moments – designing these to ensure the overall balance of the gathering is positive, and participants leave with a good feeling – those redemptive stories we explored in Chapter 2.

Vary energy levels throughout the day; balance high-energy moments with action-oriented moments and connection moments. And leave white space; people need reflection, quiet work spaces, wellness zones and meditation lounges.

Design inclusively: ensure physical and sensory accessibility, create programmes that work for everyone – neurotypical and neurodiverse. Consider sensory planning for varied attention spans and balance formats; no one wants eight 40-minute sessions.

Master the transitions between sessions – avoid dead time with visual cues and lighting shifts to signal transitions. And for multi-day events build in recovery time: mindful moments, recharge zones with hydration stations, tech charging areas and comfy seating. And space for social resets. Quiet zones.

The art of event design is to design moments – touchpoints – including peak moments,[10] as well as whole experiences. But sometimes they just happen.

Penny Mordaunt, a former British Conversative politician, served as the Lord President of the Privy Council and the Leader of the House of Commons, and she stole the show at the coronation of King Charles II and Queen Camilla. There was viral coverage including headlines like 'the Penny is mightier than the sword.'

In her role as Lord President of the Privy Council, she performed a ceremonial role in the proceedings, carrying an 8lb, four-foot 17th-century Sword of State into Westminster Abbey during the King's Procession. The sword represents the king's authority, and she was holding it upright for an hour.

Reflecting on it later, she talked about how a member of the royal family wrote to her after the coronation saying 'it was so kind of the King and Queen to come to your event.'

Those peak moments have the ability to change how people feel. Previously perceived as a 'former Conservative leadership hopeful' – Penny had tried for the party leadership twice – even losing her seat in the landslide 2024 Labour election win didn't dull the shine on her newly minted reputation.

Recruiting speakers and talent

We've all seen the speaker arriving, delivering one of their three canned presentations and rushing off to their next appointment without any engagement.

When you build authentic, enduring partnerships with speakers, there's a qualitative difference in the results. Whether that's their pre-event excitement and sharing on socials, their commitment to the programme or recommending other hard-to-reach speakers.

Aim for a speaker line-up as diverse as your audience, nurturing opportunities for upcoming talent.

Optimizing content

When you spend time with your speakers fine-tuning their content – whether it's a short presentation, fireside chat, contribution to a panel – that investment shows in the quality of the live content.

Understanding their motivation

I've often likened recruiting event speakers to a headhunter role. And here's why: to secure the best speakers, you need to be able to put yourself in their shoes like all the best sales people.

What's the speaker's motivation? Why do they want to give up their time and headspace? Particularly if they're not being remunerated. But even if they are, paid speakers and talent are usually sought after, so you'll still need a compelling pitch.

One of the most powerful pieces of value you can offer speakers is the behind-the-scenes Green Room connections. When I've hosted the CTOs of NASA, the UN and the *Financial Times* for a post-conference dinner, the connections they forge create long-lasting and personal impact.

Ensuring a transformational event for your speakers means that they'll always want to work with you.

How can your event be transformational for your talent?

For your event to be impactful, it's no longer enough to just secure the speaker. What your speakers and presenters say is at the heart of the impact of your event, and collaborating with and guiding them is crucial.

Dame Steve – Stephanie – Shirley is an inspirational tech pioneer, entrepreneur and philanthropist. Born in Dortmund, she arrived in the UK in 1939 on the Kindertransport as a refugee from Nazi Germany.

She worked in the Post Office Research Station in the 1950s, building computers and writing machine code, studying for a maths degree at night school. She went on to found an all-women software company, pioneering remote working. It was ultimately valued at almost $3 billion, and it made 70 of her staff millionaires. It later became Xansa and is now part of Sopra Steria Group. She donated most of her wealth to charity, and since 'retiring' her work has been in philanthropy, with a focus on autism and IT.

I asked Steve what makes an event powerful and impactful.

She replied that professionalism makes the biggest difference – and told me this story.

> *I spoke at TED in Vancouver in 2015 to some 1,200 international IT leaders and got a standing ovation. Some months before, I had not known what a TED talk was. Its impact on my profile was immediate, it has been viewed over 2 million times and continues to attract about a thousand more views every month.[11]*

> *But it's the professionalism that made it so special for me. First a video run-through, with an active critique. 'We want this to be the very best presentation you have ever done.' Then when I got to Vancouver, another run through. Only when it was for real did the audio go dead on me not once but twice. The audience was very much on my side before I even got started.[12]*

Saying thank you

Appreciating speakers and talent is important – whether they are paid professionals or not. To get the best out of your speakers, you'll build a personal connection with them. They have invested time and insight in creating live content that's bespoke to your gathering.

And in my experience, many of the greatest professionals still have a moment of nervousness before they go on stage to a big audience.

An immediate and personal thank you is always appreciated. Please don't mail merge your generic thank you a week later. I tend to send mobile voice notes in the cab back from the event –

whatever time it is – I'm still on the event high, and speakers seem to appreciate the genuine personal note and often comment on how inspired I still sound.

Advisory boards and content committees

The terms Advisory Boards and Content or Programme Committees are often used interchangeably; it's helpful to differentiate them as they're based on diametrically opposed design thinking.

Programme Committees

Many medical and scientific societies have honorary, often elected, programme committees that collaboratively shape event content.

While there are sometimes academic papers to review for presentation and Programme Committees can bring a wealth of experience, technical expertise and depth of knowledge, in my experience, this approach can result in generic outcomes.

Additionally, they may not have a sense of the larger competitive marketplace or review their themes or tracks in light of bigger drivers and trends. The art of curating a compelling conference programme requires an ability to be both inside and outside the market; ask the tough questions and build content differentiation into the final output.

Some Programme Committees start by reviewing last year's agenda, cutting sessions to make room for new, ad-hoc ideas. This approach risks groupthink and stifles creativity. Indeed, I believe that the consensus-driven approach of committees leads to poorer content. Your committee members may enjoy the process, but the programme may suffer.

While this approach has long worked, in competitive markets, its lack of rigour can have a detrimental effect on an event's success. Programme committees, while sometimes including 'early career' members, are often composed of seasoned professionals and may unintentionally overlook the broader needs of younger or more diverse members.

Volunteer committees are vital, but some fail to engage newer audiences or keep pace with commercial competitors. It's time for association Chief Event Officers to step up – taking a lead on content strategy rather than simply following the guidance of respected but traditional committees.

Advisory boards

Advisory boards serve a different role – less formal, typically handpicked by the programme director and designed to reflect the market while featuring industry rock stars.

They're a marketing asset, allowing you to announce their formation before the programme even exists. Board members' networks also help connect you to your audience. Inviting respected leaders as a 'low touch' role – offering promotion, Green Room access and speaker connections – creates a valuable exchange.

Build an advisory board that mirrors your Market Map, ensuring diverse perspectives. Aim for big names, pitching it as a low-investment no-meetings commitment – just direct input to the content and some easy kudos. A pre-event dinner can add connection and networking value. Prioritize accessible, proactive members who share connections and get things done over those who defer to endless meetings.

Your content plan

Bringing together your reading, research calls, survey data, responses on social is something of an alchemic act. You understand your market and its needs; you have data on recent trends and latest developments, and you also have an understanding of which speakers will connect with participants personally. You know which left-field topics will ignite great debate, who are the speakers who will have participants queuing.

Event design is a catalytic moment. Use the principles of design thinking to design, prototype, collaborate, test and iterate. Combine this with tools from user experience – UX – such as the

Empathy Map, understanding what you want your participants to think, feel, say and do.[13]

⬇ Starting with a **Content Flat Plan** – a large grid showing both physical space and time – map your hard and soft content, deciding upfront which to prioritize. This will shape your event; is it driven by the big presentations or the connection opportunities? Sharing and iterating is a crucial part of the research process, so feedback is vital.

Have the Peak End Rule in mind; people tend to judge an experience primarily by its most intense moment (the peak) and how it ends, rather than the entire experience. You can design this; think deeply who to open and close with, and which parts of the experience to privilege.

Your content might require collaboration across your organization; content sits in different parts of the org chart, depending on the type of event company as well as other factors. Corporates don't always have control of the content and may be working with business or corporate affairs teams. Associations often have content committees. Trade shows often partner with associations or other external organizations, who may have content expertise, but may not always have *event* content expertise.

Pureplay conference companies start with content; other commercial and media-owned events have content at the heart or work closely with editorial – which has its challenges, depending on the journalist.

Wherever your content sits in your organization, content is not a commodity. As a Chief Event Officer, I invite you to get as close to the content as you can; explore it, interrogate it, put yourself in your attendees' shoes and interrogate it on their behalf.

From content to experience

You've mastered content research and have a checklist of the range of different content types, an insight into the hard and soft content concepts, and an understanding of how to work with advisors and maximize your speaker relationships. Bringing all this together into the Content Flat Plan will help you structure your initial event design.

The next steps are to understand how to interweave these building blocks with ideas from the world of experience design.

Chapter 7
Crafting the experience

We are all the product of our experiences, and crafting the gathering experience adds another dimension to your event.

My mum is what would nowadays be called a creative; she's a pianist by training, with a brilliant eye for design and basically just fabulous taste. I grew up in a house filled with mid-century modern and seventies design icons. Our purple seventies living room (we had a purple seventies, some people had a brown seventies) had at its centrepiece an Eero Saarinen X Knoll Tulip Table, and I was inspired by its organic curves and simplicity.

The table designer Eero's father, Finnish designer and architect Eliel Saarinen, has something to teach us about curating the gathering experience and event design – 'always design a thing by considering it in its next larger context – a chair in a room, a room in a house, a house in an environment, an environment in a city plan.'

And as a Chief Event Officer, you will design your moment within your experiences, the activations within your shows and the experience within the context of your vision and purpose.

You've internalized the building blocks of creating your event content: hard content, soft content, creating belonging and community, building relationships with your speakers and talent, working with advisory boards and developing a content plan.

Now it's time to take that to the next level. As the world of events and gatherings develops, it has crashed head on into the world of experience design.

Experience design is a relatively new field,[1] taking its cues from museums, cultural experiences, improv theatre, the creative arts, website UX design, science and neuroscience, and learnings from associated fields such as brand marketing and retail activations.

Event professionals understand that to grab participants' attention and engagement, to create those memorable moments that help create transformation, event design has a huge amount to learn from the world of experience design.

A case in point.

The London Motor Show, once the UK's biggest trade events, ran from 1977 to 2019. For decades, it was the go-to stage for car launches from the likes of Jaguar and BMW. But, ultimately, it stagnated. As one industry veteran put it, 'just cars on carpet with promo staff'. The world evolved; the show didn't.

Enter Lord March and the Goodwood Festival of Speed in 1993 – a high-octane antidote to automotive complacency. His mission? Bring motorsport back to the Goodwood estate and revolutionize the experience. Goodwood wasn't just a show; it was an experience. Live action replaced static displays: cars roaring up the Hillclimb, F1 pit lane access, future tech showcases and the immersive Electric Avenue. As Media 10's Rob Nathan said, 'Automotive brands didn't want the NEC anymore. Festivalisation transformed the sector.'[2]

The formula worked. Goodwood Revival followed in 1998 – vintage cars, period dress and a celebration of craftsmanship that predated throwaway culture. It's a living, breathing time warp with a modern message of sustainability.

Then came Goodwoof in 2022 – a dog-centric festival of agility trials, demonstrations and tail-wagging joy, all sprinkled with the Goodwood magic.

Goodwood isn't a motor show; it's a masterclass in brand evolution and experiential impact. You're not just a spectator; you're part of the experience.

This chapter explores ways to engaging with participants emotionally, intellectually and sensorially, to create unique and valuable gathering experiences.

Rules of engagement: the experience economy

It's over 25 years since Joe Pine and James Gilmore coined the term 'experience economy'.[3]

That's changed your life and mine in how we experience brands – think how coffee shops have evolved from commodified dispensers of undifferentiated cups of coffee to how Starbucks created the 'third place' where you might easily take your laptop and work for a couple of hours, while sipping an expensive coffee that was delivered with a degree of theatre and the faux sense of personal connection.

Have you been to Kidzania? A mini world where children role-play adult jobs and earn kidzos currency. It's a genuine learning experience; I remember the moment my seven-year-old realized the Kidzania cash machine didn't give out free money – it was *his* money, that he'd earned. The ensuing realization that it wasn't free money spitting out of the real bank's cash dispenser but my hard-earned cash – the shock on his face said it all.

As a family we've shared some revelatory experience-led trips.

Washington's International Spy Museum invites visitors to become undercover agents; you're assigned a new identity, receive an undercover radio frequency identification (RFID) badge and receive a series of tasks and missions to test your spy skills as you explore the exhibition. You create a disguise and build your own spy gadget – and receive your personalized debrief via email when you leave.

The Lego House in Billund, Denmark, is both a brilliant example of experience design and our most talked about family holiday. It lives its values – as you approach it in a residential area, there's an enormous, well, Lego house. Twenty three metres tall and designed by Bjarke Ingels Group, the clay tiles were designed to Lego brick scale and colours, creating the illusion of 21 floating LEGO bricks.

Its six colour coded zones seamlessly blend experiences, creativity, play and immersive storytelling, and you are definitely the hero of the story. It's all about you from the moment the Lego staff welcome you like enthusiastic youth leaders helping guide you on your personal journey. The house's value proposition of 'inventing the future of play' was brought to life, energizing us all to play and create. The Mini Chef Family restaurant is truly experiential – you place your order by selecting Lego pieces from a tiny four-piece set, building a shape you then slot into the 'computer'. A personalized animation takes you through the process, reminding you when your order will be delivered by the robots on the track coming from the kitchen.

And, of course, your (quite delicious) lunch is delivered in – yes you guessed it, Lego-shaped insulated lunch boxes. It's one holiday mealtime that was full of fun and excitement. And you got to take home your mini-order Lego, and the kids got a Lego minifig chef as a gift.

The experiences designers at the Washington Spy Museum and the Lego House and team members at Walt Disney Imagineering – who create the Disney World experience – all share some design DNA with Chief Event Officers and gathering experience designers.

But these experiences are a far cry from the gamification you sometimes experience at events. This is not a card you get stamped by exhibitors with a prize at the end. The challenge for Chief Event Officers is to explore when and how to invest in experience design, for which elements of the event, and how it can add value and deliver your event's vision.

Pine and Gilmore recognized experiences as a distinct economic offering and explored how brands and businesses could leverage this thinking to create significant business growth. We, the customers – and our participants – are increasingly in search of experiences that resonate on a personal level to create lasting memories.

This can work brilliantly for brands creating event activations; take Cannes Lions. Originally inspired by the Cannes Film Festival, The Cannes Lions International Festival of Creativity is the world's largest celebration of creativity in communications. It's truly a 5Cs gathering combining connection and community, learning and awards in a beachy festive atmosphere.

The 2024 festival delivered immersive brand experiences in spades – designed for entertainment – and a long tail of user-generated content.

Instagram's *Devlin's Reels Cinema*[4] showcased *There Is No Other*, a 9:16 vertical short film on the transformative power of human connection. Pinterest's Manifestival turned the platform into a life-sized, picture-perfect playground. Spotify Beach offered daily jam playlists, concerts, DJ sets and the celebrity-studded Spotify Soirée (prime for Instagram celebrity shots). Netflix brought *Emily in Paris* to life with a branded boulangerie serving themed bread and coffee.

The *Wall Street Journal*'s Journal House featured a WSJ Bistro where table mats were actual newspaper pages. And LinkedIn's The Place to B2B blended immersive entertainment with fresh Bain & Company insights into the $18 trillion B2B market.[5]

Pine and Gilmour present the Progression of Economic Value, which forms an Economic Pyramid, a succession of offerings, built on the ones below, starting with:[6]

- Discover and extract **commodities** (undifferentiated products)

- Develop and make **goods** (distinctive, tangible things)

- Devise and deliver **services** (activities the business performs)

- Depict and stage **experiences** (the feeling customers get by engaging with the business)

- Determine and guide **transformations** (the benefit customers/guests receive by spending time there)

As event designers, the experiences and transformations offering resonate the most – we've moved on from commodities and goods – and how we can speak to our participants through this lens.

The new rules of engagement: *The Transformation Economy*

In his forthcoming book, Joseph Pine argues that transformations are a distinct economic offering.[7]

Pine says 'The economic function of transformations is not to change, modify, or regenerate, but to *guide*… to come alongside customers and do everything you can to lead, steer, direct, encourage, urge, persuade, cajole, and anything else required to foster aspirants along the path they desire, and pay you to achieve.'[8]

Pine outlines four levels of experience, culminating in the transformative.

Four levels of experiences

- Memorable: basic level of engagement, connects who we are

- Meaningful: significantly connects with who we are

- ▸ Transporting: take us out of ourselves – gives us awe, gets us into flow, delivers peak experiences

- ▸ Transformative: experiences that change who we are, helps achieve our aspirations

Pine said to me: 'The transformation is going to truly happen afterwards. Until you reflect on and integrate it into your life, it's not going to be sustained through time. The transformation is geared towards having people help each other in a sustaining way, having accountability.'[9]

A valuable insight for Chief Event Officers is to design experiences with impact *beyond* the event. Create post-event avenues for participants to support each other, fostering lasting transformation.

HLTH, founded in 2018 by Jonathan Weiner and acquired by Hyve in 2024, stands at the intersection of healthcare innovation and societal well-being, and pitches itself as 'healthcare reimagined'. Its three pillars are events, community and foundation. The HLTH Foundation promotes equitable and inclusive healthcare and leads initiatives to deliver this. These programmes sustain the transformation: the follow-through is the best way for participants to both create impact and engage with the community.

In the corporate sphere, just as a film director harmonizes the contributions from a vast array of specialists, a brand director brings together the lessons of street theatre, improv, arts and creativity to create an immersive experience.

And like our master chef/artist in Chapter 2, the Chief Event Officer synthesizes a whole team of creatives to bring the vision to life. A key lesson from Pine and Gilmore is that 'transformations go beyond just creating memorable experiences to actually changing the customer'.

As Chief Event Officers, we craft experiences that shape participant emotions and guide transformations, ensuring our guests achieve the change they seek.

Art and science of designing emotions

As Maya Angelou said, 'I've learned that people will forget what you said, people will forget what you did, but people will never forget how you made them feel.'

How you make people feel is at the core of experience and emotion design.

Psychologist and behaviour economist Daniel Kahneman suggested that there are two models of thought; System 1 is fast, instinctive and emotional and about intuition and instinct, and System 2 is slower, more logical and about rational thinking.[10]

System 1 accounts for approximately 95% of our daily cognitive ability, leaving the balance for System 2 thinking. So surely we'd want to design experiences that reach the intuitive and instinctive part of our cognition?

For example, I loved the beach at the British Small Animal Veterinary Association Congress in Manchester. They created a playful space to pause and reflect on the conversations and learning so far, and also a place that gave the many parents attending the event with babies in tow a brief respite. Totally reached the intuitive, System 1 part of my brain. And the relaxed atmosphere and beach toys created the ideal environment to fall into conversation with other beach goers (aka vets).

Pigalle Tavakkoli, founder of the School of Experience Design, has produced transformative experiences for cultural, scientific and commercial clients for 15 years. She talked to me about the art and science of designing emotions.[11] Based on neuroscientific research, she points out that instead of being driven by conscious thoughts, humans are driven primarily by unconscious thoughts and emotions. She says, 'In place of, "I think therefore I am", it might be more accurate to say, I *feel* therefore I am.'

She elaborates, 'emotionally charged experiences lie at the core experience design. Emotional information bypasses the frontal cortex, where conscious and rational thoughts are processed, and instead goes directly to the amygdala, where emotions are processed. The amygdala then sends messages to the hippocampus for memories to be formed.' When we design emotional events, there is a resonance which activates memories, so that the events will be memorable, impactful and long-lasting.

Pigalle shared a case study from her role as Head of Experience at Guerilla Science, who devise entertaining and unforgettable experiences for innovative ways to discover science. *The Intergalactic Travel Bureau* created by Guerilla Science, is a pop-up travel agency with role-playing intergalactic travel agents to help you plan your next holiday to outer space. Space science researchers, such as a quantum physicist or an astrobiologist, accompany the travel agents. The actors facilitate questions and dialogue with the researchers for non-hierarchical, two-way dialogue to take place between non-specialist public and scientists. Instead of being academic or complex, instead it's playful, fun and participatory while delivering educational content.[12]

Intergalactic Travel Bureau has toured the UK and USA, reached audiences of over 5,000 and been developed across multiple platforms such as a book and a virtual reality app and a stage show.

Pigalle says:

> *happiness is a short spike in emotion. We often feel happy in relation to a contrasting emotion. If we are consistently happy, this emotion plateaus, becomes predictable, and even dips to become boring. Our skill as an experience designer is to strike a balance between positive and challenging emotions for emotionally nuanced journeys. When we find this sweet spot, the range of emotions leads to longer-lasting memories.*[13]

Pop-up models like this require a depth of research and expertise, paired with theatre and improv skills. Imagine how you could use this as inspiration for your event or gathering.

The skill of the Chief Event Officer is to take the learnings from the world of visitor experience, education, consumer brands and apply them thoughtfully to our gatherings.

People are more likely to have those emotionally charged moments that reach their amygdala and ultimately create elevated, memorable experiences. And they're more likely to return to your events or engage further with your brand.

How do you hardwire belonging into your experience?

We talked in Chapter 3 about how community is a key element of your event's purpose. While content is an important part of the mix of what *brings* people to events – hearing the leaders in your field, the feeling of being a fly-on-the-wall at an intimate fireside chat, the roundup of speaker headshots that gives you serious FOMO – community and connection are what keep them there.

That sense of belonging is what touches people emotionally. The AI app that accurately suggests the top 10 people for you to connect with.

So we're understanding the science behind how powerful human connection powers events.

Oxytocin is 'the love hormone' – primarily a molecule of social connection. It affects every aspect of social and economic life, from who we choose to make investment decisions on our behalf to how much money we donate to charity. Oxytocin tells us when to trust and when to remain wary, when to give and when to hold back.

Neuroeconomist Paul Zak's lab first discovered that oxytocin is released when we feel trusted. He then pioneered the science of immersion – putting emotional spikes into experiences.

'There's a positive correlation between immersion and recall – even weeks later,' Zak told me.[14] Simply put, deeper immersion creates lasting memories.

His Immersion Neuroscience lab developed an app that tracks Key Moments – peak engagement, Value (how much an experience resonates) and Safety (psychological security).[15] Zak calls it a way to 'quantify the return on experience'.

The lab has already used its Value Measurement tools to predict Spotify streams and ad impact. Now, imagine events where both attendees and Chief Event Officers get real-time data on what truly resonates.

Employees who feel they belong are 167% more likely to recommend their company.[16] Now, imagine that at an event.

Storycraft Lab in Washington, DC, uses human-centred design to explore belonging's impact on organizations and experiences. Their work identifies eight pathways to belonging – joy, authenticity, empowerment and more – forming the backbone of their Experience Profiles.

This tool helps organizations design with empathy, going beyond psychographics. Attendees take a quiz to reveal one of six profiles – creator, explorer, thinker, harmonizer, adaptor or igniter – guiding personalized experiences.

At RainFocus Insight 2025, these Experience Profiles were integrated into the event platform, shaping networking and content recommendations for the 400 participants. 'Humans and emotions drive impactful events,' says Naomi Clare Crellin, Founder and CEO of Storycraft Lab.[17] 'That's how we make the best strategic decisions.'

Immersive experiences

Immersive experiences engage participants fully, transporting them through multi-sensory interactions and active participation. They go beyond entertainment, breaking the fourth wall and placing attendees at the heart of the story, creating a deep sense of presence and emotional connection.

Punchdrunk, founded in 2000 by Felix Barrett, revolutionized theatre with immersive storytelling. Forget passive spectators – audiences wander in dreamlike worlds, uncovering narratives as they go. Its 'mask' shows, like *Sleep No More* (sold out New York shows for 14 years), *The Drowned Man* (which smashed National Theatre records) and Shanghai's longest-running international production, have defined the genre.

I experienced *The Drowned Man* a decade ago, *Faust* even earlier, and the journey – the staging, the puzzling nature of crafting your own story – still lingers. Punchdrunk's reach extends beyond theatre, with collaborations across music, fashion and TV, working with brands like Louis Vuitton, Alexander McQueen, HBO and Plan B Studios to create unforgettable live experiences. Their mission? To leave audiences punchdrunk – spinning, seeing stars, intoxicated by the magic.

Since 2007, London's Secret Cinema has created immersive movie worlds. Their 2025 *Grease* experience blurs the line between screen and reality – the Rydell High story unfolds around you. Live music, dancing, stunning '50s sets and costumed guests. The VIP Immersive ticket gives you a pre-show experience to learn the dance moves and take the stage. Acquired by TodayTix in 2022, Secret Cinema has been partnering with brands since 2018. These bespoke awe-inspiring events deepen fan connections and create unparalleled brand opportunities. EE Home Presents: The Circus was a family-focused immersive experience blending circus spectacle and storytelling around the 'everyday' family, The Coopers. Showcasing EE Home products and created with Havas Play, it featured performers from Revel Puck's Circus and a branded narrative highlighting six smart home benefits.

These immersive principles apply to event design. Festivalization is one approach that blends personal and professional, creating alternate worlds – where you can discuss insurance in shorts and sunglasses.

Event designer and Master of Ceremonies (MC) Samme Allen shared a transformative experience: the 2019 MPI European

Meetings & Events Conference in The Hague where Daan Roosegaarde's keynote sparked curiosity, followed by an immersive challenge – a 400-person escape room, trying to escape the Fokker terminal. And a real-world crisis management wargame, where delegates played a company hacked by Anonymous – transforming an event into an unforgettable, high-impact experience.

The scenario forced them to hone their diplomatic and persuasive skills under pressure. An event that didn't just inform, it challenged and transformed.

Breaking the fourth wall

Great event experiences break the fourth wall. When a character acknowledges the audience or that the story's fictional, in theatre, film, TV and video games.

Think of Kevin Spacey's Frank Underwood character in *House of Cards* sharing his schemes direct with you, the audience.

Or award-winning UK TV show *Fleabag*, created by and starring Phoebe Waller-Bridge. The show became something of a phenomenon in the twenty-tweens, with its masterful use of fourth-wall breaks, with Phoebe addressing the audience directly. There's also a standout scene where the 'hot priest' also acknowledges the audience, creating a meta-narrative twist.

Traditional content-led gatherings and events can be, well, traditional. The speaker is on stage and the audience are listening (or looking at their phones), with a short time for Q&A.

We know from these consumer or brand experiences how energizing and engaging alternate approaches can be. And we know that for modernity, for our attention-deficit selves, creating new ways of breaking the fourth wall can change events.

It can be as simple as an experienced speaker jumping off the stage and wandering into the audience. Baroness Eliza Manningham-Buller, former Director General of MI5 (the UK's security service), was keynoting an event I curated and did just this. When you see someone at the top of their game, it's a masterclass. She was masterful in how she held the audience of nearly 1,000 in her hands – the rapt faces, hanging on her every word and watching her every move. She's the kind of woman I'd want on my escape room team.

ISE – Integrated Systems Europe – is the annual tech show for the systems integration and audiovisual industry. It welcomes 85,000 attendees and 1,600 exhibitors to Barcelona each February, delivering a mix of free and paid-for content. The show offers a range of expert tours for different sub-markets, led by tech specialists.

These tours help break down the barriers of a huge show, guiding participants in navigating the floor and inviting them to step through the imaginary wall separating exhibitors from attendees.

The power of art

Susan Magsamen and Ivy Ross explore the intersection of neuroscience and art in *Your Brain on Art*, introducing neuroaesthetics – the study of how artistic experiences shape cognition, emotions and well-being. Their theory? Engaging in art, music and dance fosters deeper human connections, enhancing empathy and cooperation.

For Chief Event Officers, this means designing shared artistic experiences to build belonging. Whether it's the medical parody band Coldspray performing 'The Sound of Sepsis' at a clinical conference or a powerful musical opening, creativity enhances engagement.

At the British Society of Haematology's 2024 meeting, 1,500 specialists gathered and it opened with a performance by the B-Positive Choir – a group of singers affected by sickle cell, formed by NHS Blood & Transplant, Kanya King and the MOBO Awards to raise Black blood donor awareness. The rave testimonials prove it: creative experiences in events foster connection and deliver unforgettable peak moments.

Next time you're exploring a live illustrator on stage at your gathering, remember – it's more than fun; it's a powerful way to foster human connection through shared experience.

The power of play

Lego Serious Play facilitator Nico Meyer led a playful online session for the Utrecht Convention Bureau, sending participants Lego kits in advance.

The day's theme – how to grow relevance as a business events destination – unfolded in panel discussions and online Lego Serious Play sessions. Attendees built their ideas, debated in breakouts and collectively shaped solutions. All input fed into the Lego room, culminating in a visual, video-friendly recap – more engaging and crucially more memorable than any report.

I had a playful experience visiting the BMJ (*British Medical Journal*) offices. On the meeting room desk was a box of fidget and skill toys – think spinners, push-it bubble poppers and cubes. The note on the box read:

> *People often report that fidgeting with an object helps them stay focused. While research is still underway, we wanted to introduce these at BMJ for anyone who needs them.*

> *Please feel free to use these… just check whether they make sounds before stepping into a quiet zone.*

What kind of playful elements can you add to your gatherings? It might be as simple as a Catchbox throwable microphone lobbed out to the audience. Or opening your conference with creative performance. Maybe you'll invite people to your trade show stand with an on-stand Kitchen Disco hosted by your own DJ.

These playful elements hit multiple high points – they're memorable, impactful and very social-media-able too.

The elements of surprise and delight

Unexpected moments of delight – an upgrade when an attendee gets to the hotel, a personal video message from the Show Director, the staff at the dinner leaving a flower at your table because they know your dietary requirements – can all help make your gathering more memorable.

The customer experience world talks frequently about surprise and delight, and for gatherings, it needs to be baked into the experience design.

Sometimes, it's as little as a big smile and warm welcome when attendees get to the registration desk.

We can learn from the brand-aligned activities of some non-event brands.

Loading screens can be a patience test – but the *New Yorker* app turns them into a wink and a nod. As you wait, phrases like 'Checking facts...' or 'Adjusting monocle...' pop up, bound to make you grin. It's subtle, clever and proof that even mundane moments can charm with a bit of personality.

The 404 pages are digital dead ends – unless you're Lego. Their error page hits with 'Oh bricks!' and the cheeky follow-up: 'If we lose our head, we'll just snap it back on.' It's playful, on-brand and turns a moment of frustration into a genuine laugh.

Dreamforce, Salesforce's flagship event, roared back to San Francisco in September 2022 for its 20th anniversary, drawing 40,000 attendees the city's largest event since the pandemic.

The homecoming celebration was anything but subtle: Howard Street became a parade ground with a 15-piece marching band, brass ensembles, drum lines and colour guards.

'These surprise-and-delight moments create lasting memories,' said Salesforce VP Erin Oles.[18] 'From marching bands to Dreamfest concerts to spontaneous photo ops, these are the moments attendees will talk about for years.'

When leaving the Lego House, there's an enormous Lego machine, pumping out individual red brick Lego sets. This is a unique set only available at the Lego House, containing six red 2×4 bricks which can be combined in 915,103,776 different ways.[19] As I left, I received a unique card with my name and visit date, showing one possible combination – mine, as well as my own personal set of bricks. Talk about surprise and delight.

How can you explore these ideas for your gatherings? Unexpected digital gifts in the thank you email? Genuinely useful eco swag?

The power of happiness and love

We want to create memorable gatherings and one of the levers to do this is to design them to create happiness. Not unlike the redemptive stories we explored in Chapter 2.

US behavioural neuroscientist and neuroeconomist Professor Paul Zak talks about when *Time* magazine asked him for his new year's resolutions.[20]

> *I tried to summarize what I've learned, and how I live my life. I call that process Love Plus. What I try to do is to ensure that for every interaction I have, I add love to the world.*

> *Love is a peak immersion moment. When you do that the person you're interreacting with has a peak immersion moment, and that moment is contagious.*

> *So if I add love to one person, they add love to somebody else – that way we not only improve one person's life, we improve the entire world. It turns out that people who are loved, who are cared about, who have deep social connections, live longer, live happier and live healthier. That's the way to live a fulfilled life, all you need is a little love.*

Designing our experiences to ensure 'more love' – human connection – can only increase the virtuous circle of oxytocin. Whether that's architecting spaces that encourage and elevate personal conversations or as simple as asking participants to say good morning to the person sitting next to them. More intentional threads of joy, humour and conversation help participants Only Connect.

Memorable moments

Academics, futurists, social scientists and event professionals are exploring how to design peak experiences – memorable moments that leave a lasting impact. In a two-day event, not everything needs to be magical but well-placed high points ensure lasting impressions.

Stanford professor Chip Heath and his brother Dan, in *The Power of Moments*, explain why certain experiences stand out.[21] Their theory of elevation suggests peak moments are unexpected, sensory-rich and emotionally charged, often involving joy or excitement. Designing surprise recognitions, bold openings or interactive experiences makes them unforgettable. They highlight the Magic Castle Hotel in LA, a budget stay with top-tier reviews thanks to engineered peak moments – like the Popsicle Hotline, where guests order a popsicle via phone and receive it poolside on a silver tray, delivered by a white-gloved staffer.

James Wallman, futurist and CEO of the World Experience Organization, expands on peak moments in *Time and How to Spend It*, introducing the STORIES framework to identify experiences that maximize happiness.[22] His New Peak-End Rule emphasizes creating multiple peaks and savouring the end for lasting impact.

David Adler, founder of BizBash,[23] reinforces the power of high-energy moments in event design, proving that intentional peaks create unforgettable experiences.

> *I recently felt an electric charge of possibility at Brooklyn's House of Yes during the first US World Experience Summit. The room crackled with energy – that unmistakable feeling that you're standing at the frontier of the future, where the next big idea is only a conversation away. The person across the room might be your next co-founder,*

creative partner or investor. The casual chat next to you could spark the next billion-dollar startup.[24]

Collective effervescence

Émile Durkheim's theory of collective effervescence is a sociological concept describing a feeling of unity, joy and heightened emotional intensity that can occur when people come together. It's characterized by a synchronization of emotions and a shared sense of purpose.

Think of being at Lady Gaga's 'Mayhem Ball' concert at Copacabana Beach in Rio de Janeiro surrounded by 2.1 million other superfans.[25] That's collective effervescence.

Tony Robbins has been leading firewalks – walking barefoot over a bed of hot coals – for over 40 years; he describes it as a 'powerful expression of moving beyond one's fears.'

When you do the firewalk, everything is heightened: the crowd, the drumming, the energy, the group chanting and yelling creates a peak experience for most firewalkers that lasts well beyond the experience. That incredible buzz – that's collective effervescence.

While your health and safety team are unlikely to recommend firewalks, part of your event design process is to explore how you can create those moments that energize, bring people together, heighten their experience.

These core moments, people, places or activations that grab peoples' attention, gets them tweeting or sharing. Talking. Uplifted. Impacted. Changed.

Curating those moments is the difference between having 10,000 delegates or 10,000 ambassadors who love what you do and tell your stories for you. When you are lucky (or strategic) enough to curate these moments of collective effervescence, you create superfans. Your participants can't wait to sign up for the next event at this year's event. You receive phenomenal testimonials. Your event becomes that Hot Ticket that everyone wants.

Placemaking is an experience choice

Placemaking isn't just for public spaces – it's a core event design and content decision. Choosing the right location tells your gathering's story and reinforces its intentions.

Thinking like a Chief Event Officer means deliberate, purposeful planning. A mid-range hotel basement with stale sandwiches doesn't reflect strong values. If sustainability is key, your venue should have stellar eco-credentials – and you should highlight them.

Accessibility matters, too. No attendee should need assistance just to enter. The venue, its design and how you use it aren't just logistics – they're content decisions that embody your organization's and your event's values.

Don't Forget the Bubbles (DFTB) is a global network of paediatric emergency specialists who know the power of distraction (bubbles for kids). Their research is legendary – six doctors once swallowed Lego heads to measure gastrointestinal transit time. (The average found and retrieval time (FART) was 1.7 days.)

Beyond experiments, DFTB is a thriving research and training hub and the force behind the annual DFTB Live conference. In 2021, it returned to London, and we were tasked with creating a standout experience for 500 attendees. Previous events spanned two floors of the QEII Centre, but we opted for the Business Design Centre – a flexible, fully 'ownable' space for interactive activations, quiet zones for parents and prime social media moments.

The social heart? The Foundling Museum, an 18th-century refuge for abandoned children, now celebrating creativity in child welfare. Hosting the party there made DFTB's mission tangible – because for them, it's never just an event. It's a story in motion.[26]

Dundee, Scotland's fourth largest city, has faced challenges due to the decline of traditional industry, contributing to its second-highest rate of drug misuse deaths in the country.

However, it is also undergoing a £1 billion regeneration, featuring the V&A Dundee, and is recognized as a global hub for tech, life sciences and electric vehicles.

In 2015, Dundee was selected to host the 17th International Society of Addiction Medicine (ISAM) Congress, welcoming over 600 participants from 56 countries. The destination choice brought the stories and work of the clinicians to life.

There was a parallel arts and culture festival featuring works relating to issues surrounding substance misuse. The exhibition promoted interdisciplinary thinking in the fields of science, art and design, and featured artworks with links to Dundee, and facilitated wider community engagement around the Congress.

Neil Brownlee, Head of Business Events at VisitScotland, told me, 'it was about bringing the world's experts to Scotland to discuss and progress towards a solution. And in some ways, turning the benefits and characteristics of the city on its head.'[27]

Preparing to welcome your participants

This whistlestop tour of experience design has covered the origins of the experience economy, the art and science of emotion design, the power of human connection and belonging, what we can learn from consumer immersive experiences, the power of play, the elements of surprise and delight, the power of happiness and love, memorable moments and collective effervescence.

With a clear understanding of the principles of both content and experience design, the next step in the *Playbook* is to understand how to leverage all of this to create a meaningful welcome.

Chapter 8
Reimagining the welcome

The big day has arrived. You've been working towards it for months, years or weeks.

Think back to your first strategy session – exploring the transformation, journey, stories, purpose, stakeholder mapping, messaging, content and experience design. This is everything you and the team worked towards, come to life.

This is your day.

The art of the Chief Event Officer is to make it look easy, but under the hood there's a ton of moving parts.

The welcome you design and create for your gathering, those opening moments of your event, set the stage for the transformation and delivering your purpose and vision.

Your participants are your guests just as much as if they were coming to your house for a kitchen supper. When your guests arrive at your home, you're prepared. The tuna pasta bake is in the oven, the Pino Grigio in the fridge and you may even have flowers on the table. When the doorbell rings, you stop what you're doing, you open the door. You are giving them the gift of your time and attention. You smile, depending on the relationship you may offer a warm hug, you make eye contact – it's personal.

Same for your gatherings.

A well-conceived welcome guides your attendees not only on what to expect and how to get the most out of the event. A well-designed welcome carefully and subtly guides your delegates through how they're going to think and feel during the event and, importantly, what they'll do afterwards. A great welcome sets the scene for your transformation.

The moment you greet your guests, they understand that they've walked through an invisible door to the world you have created for them. Much like small children sit up and listen when they hear the opening words of a bedtime story: 'Are you sitting comfortably? Then, let's begin.'

Your gathering's most powerful element

Once guests arrive, you are inviting them into the world of your event. A powerful welcome enables them to explore the stories and journeys you have created. You are inviting them to think about the ideas they hear, connect with the people you have convened, reflect on the ideas you have curated and designed into the content.

The opening moments are where you hit the high notes.

Your welcome is where you combine all your strategy, planning and hard work. Incorporate and synthesize the best ideas from your Event Purpose Proposition and the journeys you've created for your different stakeholders.

Talk about the big vision – what you're hoping (aka what you've designed) people will get out of their attendance.

If you have a sector transformation in mind, this is the time to reinforce the message. 'Today we're starting a conversation about how to change the supply chain dynamics in the global fashion industry.' 'Now is the time to work together to develop answers to the question "how can the UK construction industry respond to the challenges of regulation?"'

A warm welcome

Your aim for your welcome is that participants turn into guests – they feel less 'oh, I go to that conference' and more 'I belong here. This is my place. This is where good things can happen.'

You want to help people feel part of the story the moment they arrive.

The city of San Diego has been hosting Comic-Con since 1979. When you walk through the streets towards the San Diego Convention Centre, you are surrounded by projecting signs hanging from the street lighting. The familiar Comic-Con eye looks down on you – you already feel like you're part of something bigger. You've arrived.

For a large international gathering – consider great branding, welcome desks and warm staff at the airport. Extra points for a participant easy badge pick-up.

When you come through to the arrivals hall in Barcelona El Prat airport after a long flight, IBTM branding welcomes you, and there's a desk to guide you on your onwards travel. And when you arrive, later and freshened up, to IBTM World in a huge hall in the Fira de Barcelona, there's live music playing at the entrance to the show floor. It's welcoming, it signals your arrival – this is a celebration of your industry.

You know the feeling; you left home at the crack of dawn, gathering your bags and laptop and think you'll look at the event programme in the airport. There are crazy queues at security. Your coffee order isn't quite the way you like it. You're uncomfortable in your middle seat on the plane.

By the time you disembark you may be slightly rested, but you may also be discombobulated and haven't yet read the many emails about how to get to your hotel.

There's a Sliding Doors moment here – two alternate experiences.

In the first, you walk through the gate, head in your phone, working out where your hotel is and how to get there. It's hotter than you expected and you're overwarm. There's a long queue for the taxi, but you finally get in a cab with broken aircon and after a few minutes, your cab driver understands where you're going. The hotel can't find your reservation. By the time it's resolved, you're wrecked and don't fancy the opening night party.

In the second, as you exit, bold conference branding greets you, sparking a sense of belonging. A friendly staffer in a branded hoodie approaches with a smile, confirms you're here for the event and walks you to the Welcome Desk. Another colleague prints your badge, confirms your hotel and explains travel options. Choosing a taxi? They guide you to the stand, where another team member ensures the driver knows your destination. A seamless, welcoming arrival.

When you arrive at the hotel wearing your badge, the reservation staff immediately say, 'Hi, welcome, you're here for the Ice Cream and Artisan Food Show, what's your name?' and find your reservation speedily. When you get to the room, there's a small welcome pack from the organizers, including treats (and possibly sustainable swag from the major sponsors). There's a handwritten postcard welcoming you to the city and the event and reminding you of the party details. Maybe there's even a small freezer-box with tiny tastes of some of the latest ice cream flavours. (And wouldn't someone love to sponsor that? Perfect example of a purposeful partnership.)

Boy, are you going to the party. If you're a party person. An ideal welcome might include different choices: a party, smaller intimate dinners, a relaxed lightly curated walk-and-talk, or small city tours where you'll get to know some people.

The point is you're a visible host. Like city tour guides with brightly coloured umbrellas and colour-co-ordinated caps. People need an anchor point when they arrive in a new place, and this is it.

The pre-welcome welcome

Priya Parker, author of *The Art of Gathering*, says 'the gathering begins at the moment of discovery.'[1] That's when your attendees get your save the date, or see the first post on Instagram or register.

The welcome begins when your participants engage with you and your gathering. Rather than the long goodbye, perhaps it's really the long welcome.

I'm thinking about the event when I'm planning my travel or checking out who else I know who'll be there. I would argue that the welcome process starts the moment I've completed my registration.

What does the confirmation say? 'We're so excited to meet you in Lisbon! Thanks for registering, your tribe awaits you' says so much more than 'I'm delighted to confirm your registration at The Venue on the Date. We'll announce the agenda shortly and send joining instructions closer to the event. Please let us know if you have any food allergies or accessibility requirements.'

Joining instructions are what event organizers send – people don't necessarily want to receive a registration confirmation, and then a final agenda email and then joining instructions. Nowadays, people mostly want one simple 'know before you go' that puts itself in the delegates' shoes, tells them what they need to know, while showcasing the personality and tone of the event and the warmth of your welcome.

While everyone loves automations, and they make life easier, I don't want to *feel* I've received an automated message. Review and refine your email copy so that your event's tone of voice and your purpose shine through. The breadth and generosity of your welcome are writ large in how you help prepare people before they attend.

For example, I was recently invited to an App Drop-In Session around 10 days before an event, designed to help me use the app well, make the right connections, plan meetings in advance and get the best out of the event. A great welcome.

Contextual welcome

Your welcome needs to reflect the context of your destination. Tessa Davis, co-founder of DFTB, the network of emergency paediatricians, told me:

> *DFTB has its heart in Australia; we've been hosting events there since 2017. Our 2023 event opened with the Welcome To Country ceremony, acknowledging the traditional owners of the land. It's a non-negotiable value, and important for us to open our event by showing respect to the Indigenous community. Everyone in Australia does this, and we honoured the Elders and took a short pause before we invited our first panel on stage.*[2]

Easy welcome

In 2007, I launched the Virtual Worlds Forum Europe, a conference and expo for a booming industry that was supposed to be 'the next internet'. Second Life was the golden child, consumer and corporate virtual worlds were emerging, and big brands were investing in a digital future. It later transpired that computing power lagged behind the vision, and the 2008 financial crash halted investment, but that's another story.

I welcomed around 600 participants and 40 exhibitors in a former Kings Cross warehouse – a venue that said tech/startup/creative. Delegates, speakers and sponsors from 30 countries gathered, making it the first European event to unite the sector. With a brilliant brand designer, we crafted a strong identity that captured the excitement of this new frontier.

Operating on a shoestring, I made it look weighty while running it from my spare room with a tiny team. Commercial events can be cashflow positive – delegates and sponsors pay upfront – which kept it viable. I invested in team t-shirts and, crucially, for rainy London in November, massive, branded golfing umbrellas. A team of volunteers lined the route from multiple Kings Cross/St Pancras exits to the venue.

All they did was hold umbrellas, smile and greet attendees: *Good morning, welcome, you're nearly there*. Simple, effective and unforgettable – tons of positive feedback.

Remember the Lego House in Billund, Denmark? The main entrance houses a 4-storey 15-metre tree made out of Lego – the Tree of Creativity (get that biblical reference?). It grows all the way up the central atrium, and you can hear the constant wows as you walk in. The tree welcomes you with a breathtaking centrepiece and anchors the start of your journey. On arrival there are energetic Lego staff, asking you how you want to spend your Lego day and talking you through your personal options. The welcome is warm and all about you, and both gives you direction and helps you navigate your day.

Generous welcome

Former restauranteur and co-producer of TV's *The Bear*, Will Guidara explores the ideas of a generous welcome in his *New York Times* bestselling book *Unreasonable Hospitality*.[3]

The book explores the lessons he learned in the hospitality business, as the General Manager, and later owner, of Eleven Madison Park, one of New York's celebrated fine-dining spots, which under his leadership gained three Michelin Stars and the number one spot on the World's 50 Best Restaurants List.

What made it a winner was Guidara's team leadership to deliver innovative cuisine combined with enabling the staff to provide extraordinary experiences, often exceeding patrons' expectations.

He highlights four tenets to the generous welcome: human connection, understanding customer needs, obsessive attention to detail and phenomenal teamwork.

Guidara says:

> *My inexperience enabled me to look critically at every step of service and to interrogate the only thing that mattered: the guests' experience. Did a rule bring us closer to our ultimate goal, which was connecting with people?*
>
> *In restaurants – and in all customer-service professions – the goal is to connect with people. Hospitality means breaking down barriers, not putting them up!… Create a genuine relationship and do what you need to in order to connect with the people you're serving.*[4]

Like all the best experience designers, Guidara has created his own gathering – The Welcome Conference – for dining room professionals to share ideas. It's now developed into a multidisciplinary hospitality symposium, convening leaders from across major industry and speakers from Fortune 500 CEOs to FBI hostage negotiators, musicians to magicians – and lots of restauranteurs.

They say, 'Our attendees believe… that hospitality is a craft that can be honed, a muscle that can be strengthened.' And a generous welcome is a skill that Chief Event Officers can also hone and strengthen.

Soft welcomes and hard welcomes

Like content, I think there's soft welcomes and hard welcomes.

A soft welcome is the first moment that someone engages with your event – registers their place and then ultimately arrives in the destination – airport, transport hub, city, hotel, space or venue.

Here, you're creating a welcoming atmosphere with your messaging, signage, personal welcome. You're saying to people, 'You're here, you're welcome, let's begin.'

The hard welcome for business and professional gatherings is when the content starts. Your big opener on stage. Your MC's welcome. The sizzle reel you play before the show opens.

Crafted well, these hard welcomes breathe primordial life into all your pre-event comms. You've done teaser videos and tons of social, talked about the big ideas, trailed the speakers and the 'networking'.

Now it's real.

Set the scene. Tell the story. Live the story.

When I opened the Virtual Worlds Forum in 2007, introducing Lord Puttnam talking about 'virtual worlds; media, entertainment, narrative, a shift from passive to interactive', I walked on stage to the Buggles' track 'Video Killed the Radio Star'.[5] The energy in the room was palpable. We were the revolutionaries, ahead of the curve, working out what our brave new world would look like.

Welcomes at scale

Welcomes can be more challenging for multi-stream events and trade shows and exhibitions. Some events are designed to ensure that all participants can fit in the biggest space. Some focus their positioning on the breadth of content, but this can be at a cost. While a smorgasbord of fabulous speakers and ideas feels enticing, you can only be in one activity at any one time. (Of course, a team might divide and conquer.)

British evolutionary anthropologist Robin Dunbar created the concept of Dunbar's number, popularized by Malcolm Gladwell's 2000 book, *The Tipping Point*. The maximum number of individuals in a society or group that someone can have real social relationships with – Gladwell called this The Rule of 150.

It may be that the future of events includes more micro-events, curated audience events, and there the welcome is easy.

But large corporate events, huge user conferences, global or regional trade shows are predicated on scale and here to stay. With 10,000, 100,000 or more attendees at some of these events, part of the promise *is* the size. This presents a more thoughtful challenge for Chief Event Officers convening these events, how to ensure a welcome at scale?

It's about bringing your purpose to life; whether that's the world's largest tractor at the entrance to the farming show, signifying you're in the right place, to the vibe and experience you design: music, performance, the bright colours of the brand, the simultaneous ping of the event app revealing that groundbreaking late speaker.

Be intentional

There are three elements to your intentional hard welcome. Ensure that you've drafted a witty and thoughtful script, and that your event MC is briefed but not over-rehearsed. You need their personality to shine through your script.

Your opening words

The opening words of your event are your purpose and transformation.

The International Telecoms Union (ITU), the United Nations' specialized agency for digital technology, has organized the AI for Good Global Summit since 2017, in partnership with over 40 UN Sister Agencies and the Government of Switzerland. The Summit brings together global leaders and innovators to harness AI for social good, working towards the SDGs.

Doreen Bodgan-Martin, Secretary General of the ITU, opened the 2024 events with a question: How do we govern technologies if we don't yet know their full potential?

Here's how you might open your event.

Welcome to the Global Lawnmower Manufacturer's Jamboree '25.

We're all in business because we want our customers to have the most beautiful, uplifting lawns and gardens.

The purpose of the next two days is to explore our twin challenges of the climate crisis and how we can solve ongoing supply chain issues to keep delivering great mowers, and delighting our customers.

I don't need to tell you we're a $25 billion industry. We've convened some of the greatest minds in the lawnmower world from over 40 countries.

The policy stream will ensure you leave with clear climate, regulatory and policy visions to explore with your regional governments. And the supply chain stream convenes every single player along the supply chain to discuss how we as an industry solve these issues in a concrete way (although we don't want anyone to pave over our beautiful lawns).

And don't forget the morning runs (on beautifully cut grass), the slow networking and the chilled drinks at the end of day one.

Welcome, you're among your lawnmower friends.

Invite your gathering on the journey

Second, invite attendees to come on the journey with you. Great gatherings break the fourth wall; it's not show and tell, it's come join the party.

So the next thing your opener does is draw people in. How can *they* change the world. Call them out, so they feel seen and heard.

Whether you're a lawnmower manufacturer or parts maker, whether you're a retailer or a comms professional dealing with the lawnmower shortage, this is your place.

Make connections. Your input counts. We'll be leaving with the Global Lawnmower Plan, and your contributions are what will help change our world.

Avoid talking about logistics at this point. This is not the place to tell them about the Wi-Fi or where the fire escape is. You might quickly point people to where the QR code is for this information on their badges or online, but now is not the time. Don't break the spell.

Obvious, I know, but I can't tell you how many events I've attended where the opportunity to convene and inspire has been lost.

Engagement upfront

Third, engage the audience straight away:

> *Please turn to the person next to you, and share your three biggest lawnmower challenges. You've got 5 minutes.*

⬇ Get people talking. Use the **Welcome Planning Grid** to organize your thinking.

Budget permitting, you might add a myriad of production elements to elevate your message. Your stage set should ideally look and feel brand-infused, with creative touches that inspire the audience.

Perhaps short video openers – but please, no lengthy sponsor videos if you can possibly avoid it.

Or you might open the event just doing the thing you're there to do. I love a Creative Open.

Laidlaw Opera Trust believes that opera holds a singular power to captivate the human spirit. It champions 'live opera for everyone, forever', and it invests in opera companies and houses who believe that opera should be part of everyone's cultural capital. Through strategic support and grants it aims to expand Opera's reach and repertoire sustainably.

By investing in the future of this cherished art form, it aims to enrich cultural landscapes nurturing the next generation of opera enthusiasts and artists.

The Trust launched its first event, The Business of Opera in 2024, creating a forum to explore ambition, innovation and leadership for the sector. Hundreds of opera professionals convened on a rainy day in London.

As a guest, it felt like many conferences: badges, lanyards, coffee, small talk before kick-off, participants greeting old friends and new.

But the opening was something special.

The room was buzzing; the event hadn't started. Latecomers were still finding their seats. And then award-winning New Zealand baritone Julien Van Mellaerts walked on the stage, took out his pipes and performed *Der vogelfänger bin ich ja* from *The Magic Flute*.

The atmosphere was electric. Opera lovers, of course. But more than that – an impactful reminder of why the audience had gathered. The magic of opera writ large and experienced live.

A great example of how the welcome shapes the event.

Following your Creative Open with the purposeful welcome is a magical combination. Open with feeling and experiencing the 'why' and then follow up with a well-crafted purposeful welcome.

MCs and stageless welcomes

Your event and content will likely have a host or hosts, depending on how many stages or areas your gathering has.

Work closely with your MC to craft a beautiful welcome. Ideally, your MC will be an experienced professional, with a TV or live events background. While you may want the leading professor in your field to chair your event, there's no guarantee that they have the stage presence, personality and experience to create the energy and excitement as well as manage the crowd.

In a multi-stream event you may stream the welcome and the opening conversations to multiple theatres or public spaces, so a strong presence is vital.

And there are gatherings with so many experience options that not everyone will *go* to the opening session. So the welcome is everywhere – encouraging the team on the first day to offer personal welcomes and help orientate attendees. Or changing the signage so the first hours or day makes it clear that people have just arrived and you're delighted they're there.

What can we learn from the cinema experience

My local cinema has the art of the welcome sorted. The Everyman Cinema in Muswell Hill is part of a small chain of art house cinemas, launched in 2000. The vibe is independent cinema with stylish interior design that gives a nod to the art deco interiors of the first cinema in Hampstead.

The ambience is one of hospitality; there are comfy chairs in the reception, low lighting, good art and sofas with blankets inside the cinema. And a cool menu, with coffee, artisan soft drinks, wine and nibbles brought to your seat.

What they do really well is that it feels personal. Before the movie starts, one of the team comes out and stands in front of the screen, sometimes with a short intro, but always with a charming request to turn your phone off. Human, but authoritative.

The cold open

Author Priya Parker introduced me to the idea of the cold open and how to use it well for events, reinforcing the idea of a powerful welcome.[6]

A cold open drops you straight into the action. No theme song, no credits, just instant immersion. It's a trick TV directors started playing with from the mid-1960s to hook viewers before they had a chance to change the channel. The idea? Hit them with something compelling right away, so they stay put instead of switching to whatever else was on.

TV's *The Office* perfected the art of the cold open. In the Casual Friday episode, the show starts with Kevin lugging a huge pot of chilli into the office. 'Everyone is going to get to know each other in the pot,' he says, before spilling it all over the carpet.

The theory of the cold open that TV producers really understood was that they were in the business of attention. You need to capture the attention first – before you get to any details.

Priya says, 'Every gathering, to be sure, has logistical demands.... But people do not need to know this information at the very first moment of your gathering. It's not that you don't need time for logistics and the like. Just don't start with them. Open cold.'

A word on closing

Like a fine dessert wine, a great gathering's welcome pairs with its closing – how do you complete the circle? How do you bring the narrative to a satisfying close?

We want attendees to carry the warmth of the community home, continuing the conversation through post-event salons, Discord or Slack groups, or professional networks like LinkedIn. The goal? Turning them into ambassadors and superfans. Inspiring action and transformation.

At live events, I often guide teams to capture key ideas in a shared document – because no one can be everywhere. Your role as Chief Event Officer is to connect these insights to your original Event Purpose Proposition. Then, craft a real-time script for your MC, sending it straight to their iPad, ensuring a powerful, meaningful close that highlights the best ideas.

Remember the Business of Opera event? The Laidlaw Opera Trust team also did some smart things to close the event, including asking participants to reply to the 'thanks for coming email' with one idea they wanted to share with everyone else. This became a co-created ask-the-audience takeaway for people to reflect on.

Doreen Bodgan-Martin's closing statement at the ITU's AI for Good Global Summit was equally powerful: 'We are the AI generation. This is our moment. It's our responsibility to write the next chapter in the great story of humanity and technology.' Now that's quite some call to action.

Next steps

We've worked through the *Playbook* steps to design your event; transformation, journey and story, purpose, mapping, messaging, content, experience and welcome.

The final of the initial four questions is – how do you evaluate your gathering's impact? You've had the full event experience; now it's time to evaluate if it delivered.

PART 4

HOW DO YOU BUILD IMPACT BEYOND THE EVENT?

Chapter 9
Evaluating your transformational outcome

The last big question of *The Chief Event Officer's Playbook* asks two vital subsidiary questions about the impact of your transformational gatherings.

Neuroscientist Paul Zak told me, 'Events have this sacred duty to give people amazing experiences, so measurement is important. When they work, they're successful, maintain clients and people come out transformed.'[1]

Metrics matter – measuring your gathering's success helps secure future buy-in and investment from your senior leadership.

First, we ask how do you evaluate the outcomes, the results, the change, the transformation? And how do you make this fit-for-purpose as a corporate strategic tool?

Nicola Kastner, CEO of the Event Leaders Exchange, a network of senior corporate event professionals, told me that measurement is the number one topic of interest – 86% of members want to talk about it.[2]

If in-person events are the number one channel globally for B2B marketing leaders[3] then we need to explore the best evaluation models.

Second, once we've understood the 'results' – and we're talking about something way more nuanced than a formula that grades your event – we can look deeper and ask how can we use this data to elevate the power of events, to leverage outcomes to communicate the strategic value of the gathering – ensuring that the conversation happens at a senior level?

Measurement is about data, technology, integrations. Sure. But evaluation is ultimately about demonstrating outcomes and that your gathering had a quantifiable and valuable impact on the business and its strategic objectives.

Your gathering at the heart of your organization

Creating a transformational event, and all the strategic thinking that underpins it, is about placing your gathering – its purpose, its participants, its experiences and its outcomes – at the heart of your organization. When event strategy is top-down, with the associated senior leadership and board buy-in, rather than bottom-up, the extended reach and breadth of influence is in itself transformational.

Jason Marantz is Director of Education and Inclusion at Hackney Borough Council, which faces high levels of income deprivation and child poverty. His team hosts the Annual Headteacher's Conference, designed for inspiration, connection and education.

Recognizing the isolation headteachers often experience, Marantz restructured the event four years ago, shifting to a format shaped by headteachers themselves, rather than the Council. The new approach emphasizes discussion over stage time. 'We listened to what people want,' Marantz said. 'The difference is enormous.'[4]

The conference fosters connections and shares local stories of resilience. In 2023, poet and broadcaster Lemn Sissay – who had early childhood experiences of the social care system, abuse and resulting mental health struggles, and was the official poet of the London 2012 Olympics – delivered a moving keynote.

He shared his experiences of foster care and social services, highlighting how his teacher was 'that one glimmer of light' who saw his potential.

These powerful stories inspired headteachers, reinforcing a sense of community. 'We're building a family of schools,' Marantz said. How are headteachers transformed? 'It's a powerful education conference. You hope they start making change tomorrow.'

The team developed a dashboard to track evaluation data: the most 'liked' parts of the day, suggestions for the following year and a one-word visual highlighting 'love', 'resilience' and 'collaboration' as key takeaways. This, combined with a slick year-on-year data analysis of bookings by sector, expenditure and the proportion of new attendees helped keep the team on track.

A meaningful event strategy aligns with your Event Purpose Proposition, creating an intentional environment that shapes participants' thoughts, emotions and, ultimately, transforms them.

Measurement attempts to evaluate that transformation; each event is unique in its purpose and vision, and so each event requires its own specific measures of success. For those organizing multiple gatherings you may want to evaluate the relative success of different events – with different purposes and intended outcomes – so you will need some standardization. While at the same time respecting and reflecting on the uniqueness of each gathering.

Does measurement work?

Recent research stated that over two thirds of event organizers say they struggle to prove the event ROI from their B2B conferences.[5]

There are those organizations who are either nervous or flat-out don't want to take the evaluation risk.

Nick Gold, founder of Speakers Corner, believes impact should be lasting, not just momentary.[6] Frustrated by the lack of measurement, he proposed an idea a decade ago: after a keynote, clients would survey attendees six months later to assess its impact. He approached three clients with this plan – they all declined.

A senior corporate event professional said to me:

> We measure all our events, a key success factor is around how much people are taking forward, are we getting ROI from an event? The only event we don't measure is the CEO's Strategy Day. Huge event, with all the board and senior leadership teams, where the CEO shares the vision for the next year. We'd like to measure, but she prefers not to. Nobody wants to hear that their event hasn't been successful. Internal events are harder to measure – client-facing events are easier.

Chloe Richardson, Head of Content at ELX, said 'senior event leaders need to stand shoulder to shoulder with the CMO or CFO, with the same level of insight and credibility. This starts with establishing your objectives, for your events and events programme, and how you measure it. Then all the other pieces fall into place.'

UK events sector leader and founder of Fast Forward 15 mentoring programme Fay Sharpe told me, 'The sales cycle is not "do an event – win a piece of business". Events are the beginning of building a relationship; sometimes people forget where a piece of business originated from. Three years later, someone calls you in and you win a £4m contract.'

We'd all like to find a methodology that measures more than the lasting impression, takes a nuanced approach to Key Performance Indicators (KPIs) and ROI – each event has a complex web of transformations and outcomes to potentially evaluate.

When to ask?

Most event data is collected through technology: apps, badge scans, event platforms, sometimes supplemented with qualitative research. But when's the best time to send a post-event survey?

At Informa, where my team ran over 100 conferences annually, we had a system. After lunch, paper evaluation forms were distributed, and the event chair would ask everyone to take a few minutes to complete it. It was also incentivized – all completed forms went in a prize draw. Once people started, most finished.

Regardless of when the event wrapped, I read every form that day – still riding the event high, absorbing near-instant feedback. Who shone? What didn't land? What new topics sparked interest? (A crucial product development question.)

The rule was, 'call the poors'. Anyone rating the overall event poor (effectively, the bottom 25%) got a personal call the next day. These rare but invaluable qualitative conversations provided event development gold.

Also customer service gold; attendees were so surprised and delighted to hear from the 'Conference Director' (we all had overblown job titles to impress people), combined with the ensuing listening, usually turning them into a lifelong customer.

Feedback isn't just data – it's customer connection.

You might even argue that these customer service conversations are the beginning of the welcome for the next gathering.

Begin at the beginning

Evaluation criteria should be baked into your initial strategy. As discussed in Chapter 1, that first session on your transformation–journey–storytelling–purpose needs to ask: 'How will we know if this is successful?'

There's a move towards building measurement in upfront. Bizzabo's 2025 research talks about a 'shift toward intentional planning and measurable goals reflecting a broader trend of aligning event strategies with actionable insights.'[7]

Best-selling author and UK children's laureate Frank Cottrell-Boyce is leading a campaign to combat a 'recession in children's happiness' linked to declining early reading. In early 2025, he convened The Reading Rights Summit in Liverpool, uniting experts across sectors to champion every child's right to the transformative power of shared stories. Cottrell-Boyce calls shared reading 'an effective, economic health intervention' that should be universally accessible.

The measure of success is clear: how quickly can access to stories lift children out of this happiness recession?

Long-term impact

Some gatherings are designed for long-term impact.

The UK government hosted two pivotal Farm to Fork Summits in May 2023 and 2024, focused on bolstering the nation's food security and supporting the agricultural sector.

Government events are often hardwired for outcome, with event and policy professionals working in tandem.

Convening farmers, food producers, retailers, policymakers, environmental groups, scientists, academics, financial institutions, trade bodies and government the events demonstrated the government's dedication to strengthening the UK's food security, supporting farmers, and ensuring a resilient and equitable food supply chain.

Stalls in the No. 10 garden served fresh bacon butties, with enticing aromas drifting into the Cabinet meeting room. Delighted stakeholders were surprised when the entire Cabinet arrived early, creating unexpected, high-impact connections.

Outcomes included announcements on innovation and farming schemes, expanding Seasonal Workers Visas to help solve the farm workforce issue, reviews initiated in the eggs and horticulture sectors to ensure equitable practice, the introduction of a UK Food Security Index, a £75 million assistance fund for farmers to recover from flooding and enhanced supply chain regulations.[8]

Fay Sharpe shared how she led Zibrant's 2005 rebrand. 'We lived our values for six months before launch – everyone was involved. There was an integrated incentive scheme – living the values was a given.'[9]

The process began with company-wide, customer and 360-degree surveys. Some feedback was tough, prompting a full transformation, not just a logo change. With board support, new values of pride, passion, creativity, leadership and respect were developed and reinforced through a structured programme.

The rebrand culminated in a conference where a Zibrant champion, voted by staff, received a £5,000 prize. 'Two years later, we were the industry's largest agency and sold for £15.9 million – because we lived our values.'

Sharpe emphasized how this approach changed the company entirely. The rebrand wasn't just about messaging but about embedding values into the culture. 'Staff told me they left the event feeling they'd changed the world,' she said, underscoring the deep impact of aligning brand identity with employee engagement.

Measuring your event impact and legacy

There's a potentially unlimited amount of data; the trick is to see the wood for the trees, know what questions you're asking and to collate the data to create an accessible dashboard that tells the story of your event.

Brené Brown says, 'stories might just be… data with a soul' and your role as Chief Event Officer is to manage the collation and curation of the data across different platforms and methodologies, so you can tell an accurate story to the board. This story is not about the data – it's about the impact.

The majority of event professionals use post-event surveys to collect feedback and you will need to incorporate this.[10]

Colleen Bisconti, VP Events and Experiences at IBM,[11] talks about her 'Plan of Record' document, capturing everything that happens during an event. She says, 'By the end of the event day – literally by midnight – I update it with what we achieved. The full analysis comes later, but day of, we need to determine if we achieved the goals we set out to achieve or not. This immediate snapshot has built credibility with our sales leadership and SVPs.'

Nata Nambatingué, Congress & Event Director at the European Society of Cardiology, shared their sophisticated evaluation methods for ESC Congress, one of Europe's largest medical congress with 30,000 participants. Their goal? Advancing science to improve patient care. Nata explains:

> We listen to our community to stay relevant. Feedback spans three pillars: demographics, data-driven behaviours and qualitative insights. Surveys and focus groups gather 360-degree input from delegates, sponsors, faculty, and staff. One key takeaway? No more 1,000-person auditoria – smaller rooms. We're bringing back the human scale, bringing back the daylight.[12]

Julius Solaris, an events consultant and content creator says that events are 'so hot right now because we can finally attribute their impact on the pipeline.'[13] He lists five significant factors which made events measurable: event tech platforms' developments, offline tracking tools, integrations with martech software, virtual events and AI.

What to measure?

There's an enormous range of both potential items to measure and data collection methodologies.

- Attendance rates – check-in status (for free to attend events such as trade shows and some user events), new versus returning attendees

- Participant satisfaction – surveys, audience chat, reactions to your online elements

- Engagement rates – session attendance, participant connect rates, social media engagement, exhibitor stand scans, live polling responses

- Community engagement – the number of messages sent on your event app, the resulting chat volume

- Content – tracking session attendance, live in-session poll responses, feedback on speakers' skills and presentation quality, the most popular topics

- Marketing effectiveness – sales by ticket types, evaluating relative marketing channel effectiveness, revenue by promo code, website conversation rates, email marketing open and engagement rates, social media mentions

- Sales – exhibitor and sponsor metrics on sales qualified leads, pipeline generated, accounts influenced (as part of your ABM – account-based marketing strategy) or customers acquired

- Commercial measures – for commercial events, turnover by delegates/exhibitor, overall gross and net profit

Exploring measurement models

While not an exhaustive list, these are some of the methodologies that event professionals currently use.

NPS

The Net Promotor Score (NPS) – a market research metric, developed by consultants Bain & Company – measures customer satisfaction by asking the simple question: on a scale of 1–10, how likely is it that you would recommend this event to friends?

Balancing promotors, passives or detractors, it's a great 'one number' summary of your event – although often shared when it's good. One corporate CMO overseeing a number of critical events tells me 'Our NPS scores tend to be in the 9s. That's great.'

Strategic Meetings Management

Meetings Consolidation began in the 1990s in pharma, led by Lynn Ridzon at Bristol-Myers Squibb and George Odom at Eli Lilly. Debi Scholar at PwC advanced Strategic Meetings Management (SMM), driving event tech adoption (including Cvent's 1999 launch). Today, SMM is a systematic approach prioritizing visibility, ROI and business impact.

KPIs

Key Performance Indicators (KPIs) are the heartland of event measurement. Specific to each event, organizations set them at planning stage and measure a whole range of data, often in partnership with their event management platforms, most of which have analytics and KPI modules.

Customer lifetime value

Acquiring new customers (delegates or sponsors) costs far more than retaining existing ones. Calculating delegate or partner lifetime value helps event organizers prioritize retention, tailor experiences and maximize revenue by fostering long-term attendee, sponsor and client relationships.

ROI

Event ROI remains the trusted methodology for the majority of senior event professionals. The Phillips ROI Methodology™[14] created by Jack Philips of the ROI Institute, is considered the go-to approach.

However, it still remains an area of opportunity, with 70% of event professionals reporting difficulty demonstrating ROI for in-person B2B events in 2024.[15] However, there is some optimism; nearly 24% of organizers said they prioritize sales pipeline growth when planning events, followed by increasing attendance (19%) and boosting registration revenue (15%).

Return on experience

As the world of events has developed and experiences became, well, part of the experience, return on experience, ROE or ROX, are oft-heard phrases. In the business world, ROX is used as a business metric around customer, employee and leadership experiences. The World Experience Organization has an ongoing conversation to co-create an ROX guide.

Return on purpose

While there is no formal measure of return on purpose, Accenture's 2018 report stated that 'consumers act as champions of brands they believe in – and foils to those they don't.'[16] Likewise, Fortuna Advisor's 2022 report found that high-purpose brands outperformed on common measures of financial performance, market valuation and shareholder value creation.[17]

It seems that there's an opportunity to develop a Return on Event Purpose model, evaluating how much the gathering's purpose was achieved.

Return on relationships

Return on relationships (ROR) is likewise a headline measure, analysing metrics like customer lifetime value, referral rates, social media engagement, customer satisfaction and incorporating NPS.

But sometimes, the relationship outcomes are clear to all. Former *Wired UK* editor-in-chief David Rowan founded VOYAGERS – a networking, peer-support and investment community, focused on impact – which hosts two 'counter intuitive' festivals – The Heat for the climate tech world and The Fix serving the health-tech sector, both with a clear mission to create connections to enable positive outcomes.

The Heat describes itself as 'not a conference. Don't expect dull panels or crappy coffee. Climate change is too urgent a problem to waste time. Instead, we designed it to help participants make new friends, to experience science in action, to learn and share their knowledge, to inspire and be inspired.'

The VOYAGER project lives this value of positive outcomes with a website page headed 'positive outcomes from VOYAGERS', listing dozens of favourable outcomes. As they say, 'VOYAGERS is all about peer support – people in the community helping each other achieve impact.'

So while these relationships aren't measured on a data basis, they are transparently laid out for all to see. Outcomes include 'Leon shared a stage with President Obama after an introduction by Alby', 'Mehdi was introduced to senior NHS executives to present a portable diagnostics device' and 'Jack found that a VOYAGERS dinner meetup led to 3 potential business deals and 1 potential investment, totally casually.'

Evaluating media reach as a measure

Media reach is powerful – think back to the strategies you developed for your marketing in Chapter 5. Evaluating media reach is a crucial measure of event success, requiring data-driven insights to assess impact.

Advanced data analysis platforms provide customized insights ensuring a clear understanding of what resonates. Real-time analysis allows event professionals to track campaign performance, identifying what works and what doesn't. Social listening tools play a key role, offering real-time sentiment analysis to gauge audience reactions, pinpoint key talking points and measure overall campaign effectiveness. By leveraging clean, structured data with an intuitive interface, event owners can monitor conversations, refine strategies and maximize media impact across their events.

Where technology and strategy meet

There's two approaches to measurement methodologies – technology and strategy.

Paul Zak's app – SIX[18] – from the Immersion Neuroscience lab and others like it could be the future; participants install the app on their phone, and they and event teams have individual real-time data to analyse trends and responses across all participants.

Tahira Endean, Head of Program and Oli Bailey, Head of UX at IMEX, talked to me about the measurement systems used to embrace the medium of live events.[19] Leveraging a suite of technology, the show uses heatmapping data, facial analysis – scanners give sentiment scores from facial expressions and in-app badge scanning indicates direct interaction. IMEX also create a Bluetooth network enabling a location-aware app, helping participants find their pre-arranged meetings via 'blue dot' navigation and sponsors gain insights around engagement.

Another option is engaging measurement strategy consultants. Data is useful, but for some partnering with experts can help formulate clear objectives and translate them into useful outputs. Combining a strategy-led approach with event impact dashboards can demonstrate clear event value.

The bigger impact

A soft approach to evaluate the outcome of your event is to see how its content lives on.

Every single thing that happens at your gathering can be captured for posterity. The video, photography, B roll, social media activity, digital downloads, the podcasts, the infographics – this is both content marketing magic and something with a life of its own.

In a well-designed event, your content lives on in the long tail of stories you and all the participants continue to tell. The connections that turn into relationships, the conversations that turn into impactful change. Or deals. Or both.

The people experiencing your gathering and your post-event content may be inspired to have ideas, research a scientific breakthrough or fund companies.

That content you created – how do you expand the impact?

Media owners are well placed to do this: Brené Brown's 2010 TEDx talk on the power of vulnerability has been viewed over 67 million times, one of the top five TED Talks of all time. TED has a platform and audience to amplify ideas – and this shifted her work from relative academic obscurity to a mainstream following. *The New York Times* said the event gave the world a 'new star of social psychology'.

Are there amplification opportunities beyond the world of events and media?

FIFDH, the Geneva International Film Festival on Human Rights, hosts Impact Days which facilitate collaborations between filmmakers and the vast ecosystem of NGOs, policymakers and funders. There are foundations who fund the broader impact campaign of the film, rather than the film itself. There is a growing world of documentary impact campaigns; don't make the movie without plans to amplify the story and reach millions. This 360° approach could help Chief Event Officers: consider the value of media amplification upfront.

As the world of events becomes increasingly more sophisticated, there are many opportunities for the Chief Event Officer to consider.

The final step

This is the 4 pm moment on the afternoon of the second day; the end is on the horizon.

We've explored nine steps of the *Playbook* – now to put all that strategy in the context of your organization.

Chapter 10
Making events a board-level conversation

Chief Event Officers are visionaries. The masterminds behind gatherings turn moments into meaning. Profound experiences where ideas are ignited and exchanged, where connections bloom and flourish and where momentum builds towards action.

Now is the time to leverage that expertise for the good of the entire organization.

We've been on a journey

You and I, we've been on a journey together – like an event. I hope the coffee was good.

I welcomed you at the start of the book with the question 'Why do Chief Event Officers matter?'

I talked about the genesis of a new board-level conversation – how will we best use our events to help us deliver on our bigger purpose?

Together, in these pages, we've explore the Four Big Questions. Why are you creating this event? Who is the event for? What will the event experience be? And how do you build impact beyond the event?

Now it's time to draw proceedings to a close and create a satisfying conclusion to the narrative arc.

We've explored transformation

We've unpacked who your event transformation serves: individuals, organizations or the wider industry or sector.

We've examined the ideas of journey, narrative and storytelling, and how you can apply these to your gatherings.

I've guided you through the ten principles of the *Playbook* and how you can use this blueprint, in your own unique way, to create your gatherings.

This *Playbook* gives you a framework for your event and event strategy. To curate energized, exciting events that speak to your participants and partners, your speakers and talent. That communicate your values to your workforce and your supply chain.

Purpose at the heart of your gatherings

I invite you to put your big purpose and the vision that it articulates at the heart of your gatherings.

As Eliel Saarinen advised in relation to design principles, consider placing your gatherings and their purpose at the centre of your bigger event strategy. And put your event strategy at the heart of your organization or business strategy.

The *Playbook* strategies will help you create your unique event, where you've listened to the participants and combined those insights with your organizational strategy.

That event is designed so that your audience and organization are uplifted, energized and ready to take action – for themselves (learning, developing), for their organization (relationship development and sales) and for their industry – the changes that need to happen. You have a clarity of outcome in mind as you design your experiences, content, spaces.

Events at the heart of your organizational strategy

This thoughtful approach is engineered to put events at the heart of the organization's strategy.

Events need to be a first thought, not an afterthought.

When events work hand in hand with business objectives there's clarity on what success looks like, and how you'll evaluate it.

Strategic event programmes emphasize strategic value over cost savings and compliance. Mathieu Bidamant of Amex GBT Meetings & Events says, 'Today's programs use data to align meetings and events with corporate objectives and they provide key stakeholders with visibility into how meetings and events drive business outcomes through reporting and analysis.'[1]

When you align the trifecta of transformation, journey and purpose, when you deeply understand where your events sit in the constellation of your competitor world, when you understand your stakeholders, you've mapped your market and have clarity on your messaging and how you'll deliver it, you've got a strong strategic base.

Major events needs to start with executive and board buy-in – engaging those senior stakeholders upfront starts a process that ensures your event strategy meets business objectives and can ultimately deliver meaningful outcomes.

Powering your organization's success

Great events people understand the whole organization.

They have a web of relationships inside the company to deliver meaningful events.

They know the strategy and vision teams because the best events weave a red thread of organizational messaging into the stories they tell.

They know the sales and marketing teams, who help amplify the event messaging. They know your field marketing and membership teams, who are talking directly to your customers, clients and members.

They work with your comms team, understanding the stories you're telling. They have a deep relationship with your finance and operations teams – to ensure the event delivers on budget or delivers profit and is executed expertly. They collaborate with your public affairs team to align your message with the bigger picture.

They rely on your product development teams to share expertise on your product or service so they are expressly or subtly hard-wired into your event experience.

The events team – whatever their job title – have a depth of insight that means they are ideally placed to have a significant impact on the business and participate in those bigger, strategic conversations.

What change will you make?

Events are increasingly a critical component to organizational success; they grow relationships, they build community, they inspire participants to think more deeply about your ideas.

How hard is it to know what's genuine online? The growth of generative AI has commodified content and content marketing. It's perversely made it even harder to find thoughtful, useful insights. How do you know what to trust? How do you know what's real?

Over two thirds of event strategists consider live events the most impactful marketing channel – it's where authentic, face-to-face connections are made and grown.[2]

Where attendees find genuine, unfiltered human connection.

Expertly conceived gatherings are communities. We – and our participants – are seeking belonging: to find our people, our tribe. And community – those connections that ultimately help us find meaning.

It's this deep sense of community and meaning that delivers value to organizations and transformation to sectors.

By doing this, you are in a position to make genuine, transformational change. When there's an end to siloed services, when events teams are no longer order takers, but considered business strategists, boards and senior management will reap the rewards of trust in their Chief Event Officer.

The conversation round the boardroom table

It's time for senior event professionals to become trusted advisors to the board.[3]

Whether you're a Chief Marketing Officer or other board member or senior leader, I invite you to investigate how gatherings can help accelerate your strategic goals. You may be exploring brand building, supporting your comms strategy or creating events to deliver specific strategic targets.[4]

The events sector is booming: in the UK, around 2,000 event management graduates enter the workforce annually, as well as hundreds of event apprentices each year.[5] There's an enormously diverse range of sub-sectors where people can get event experience starting out. The pickings are ripe for you to hire the best talent for your events team.

And the time is right for you to listen to your senior event professionals – your Chief Event Officers – skilled executives, deeply embedded in your organization and ideally placed to help you deliver your strategic business objectives.

The rise of the Chief Event Officer is more than a title – it's a transformation.

If you shape or aspire to shape your event business strategy, embrace the Chief Event Officer mindset, engaging with the CMO, CEO and senior executives. Speak the language of business and talk about the difference events can make.

No one gets promoted for knowing how many croissants to order. Elevate your role. Position yourself as a trusted advisor. Act as a consultant, helping the board and senior executives articulate needs, identify roadblocks and ultimately demonstrate the value your events bring to your organization's success.

The call to adventure is clear: will you step up, own your expertise and lead? The future of business is shaped in the moments we create – and no one understands that better than you.

This is it

The welcome is mirrored by the closing. The final gala. Like the hero in Campbell's The Hero's Journey, event leaders have crossed the threshold, stepping beyond logistics into strategy, influence and impact.

Sam Altman of OpenAI said, 'I think there is going to be a premium on human in-person, fantastic experiences. I can see that becoming a very huge [job] category of something new that we do.'[6]

The future is bright. The gatherings await you.

Just like the best marketing copy ends with a CTA – call to action – this book ends with an invitation: how will you, personally, uplevel the events conversation so that strategy can deliver results?

The time is now. The events industry is growing exponentially. The value that gatherings bring is clear. The pace and progress of change in the last four years has demonstrated that strategic event professionals are here to stay. Chief Event Officers can guide your organization to success, through the medium of gatherings.

Momentum is building – the time is right for a movement of Chief Event Officers. Come join us.

Acknowledgements

Like events, writing a book is something of a team effort: I have a lot of thank yous.

My family – Darren, Josh and my niece Hannah – who have been my first readers and perceptive commentators. They've put up with framework versions on the fridge, immeasurable, rambling conversations about event strategy and have given me the gift of truly quiet space. Josh, your astute comments helped shape some key ideas. You all helped make this a better book. Thank you.

My community – friends and neighbours whose generosity of hospitality and understanding gave me headspace to be head down on the book – thank you.

Alison Jones, my publisher, and I first discussed this book six years ago. Thank you for your guidance as my ideas developed and challenging me with a brilliant mix of rigorous clarity and kindness. The phenomenal Practical Inspiration Publishing team – Shell Cooper, Michelle Charman, Nim Moorthy – thank you for your attention to detail and care.

I was inspired in my early career by Marjorie Maws and Ros Oxley – two tough, no-nonsense remarkable women who taught me a huge amount about events and business. I often think, still, what would Marjorie/Ros do? And my first event industry work colleague – the razor-sharp Susanna Kempe – we have had a 30-year conversation about strategy, events, purpose and marketing… and a very lot of coffee. Thank you all.

My early readers Deborah Barleggs, Sarah Williams, Jackie Horn, Zahavit Shalev and Alyssa Gilbert, shared wisdom and a range of perspectives that helped hone my thinking.

Valuable feedback from event professionals Abi Canons, Becks McRobb and Gina Kay as the manuscript developed helped make this a significantly better book than it might have been.

I appreciate the generosity of the 100+ gathering, experience and other related professionals I spoke to while researching this book. While many of the case studies have made it into the final cut, very many excellent events and real-world examples didn't, and I look forward to finding other avenues to share them in the future.

Uri Berkowitz, conceptual designer and creative visionary, created both the beautiful cover and the infographic 'Event Transformation Blueprint' – thank you for your masterful advice and bringing my ideas to life more beautifully than I could ever have imagined.

My dear friend Michael Isaacs, copywriter, writer and thinker extraordinaire, read and commented on nearly every word in this book. Thank you – your depth of insight and wit kept me going through many long writing months.

Of course, despite the teamwork, any errors or omissions in this text are entirely mine.

And, finally, my deepest love and gratitude to my family. My parents – Charmian and Charles – gave me the gift of education and brought me and my siblings up in a book-lined home, always encouraging curiosity and knowledge. I would not be the person I am without you.

This book would not have been possible without the loving support, feedback, affirmation and endless cups of tea from my husband, Darren. You are my person – my best friend, confidant, sounding board, finder and love. The years with you have made me a better, kinder, more insightful person. This book would not exist without you; thank you. I dedicate this book to you and Josh.

Notes

Preface

[1] $1,227.3 billion according to *The Events Industry Global Market Report* from The Business Research Company. Available from www.thebusinessresearchcomp any.com/report/events-industry-global-market-report [accessed 5 May 2025].

[2] Conversation, 28 February 2025.

Introduction

[1] *Bizzabo State of Events & Industry Benchmarks* (2025) surveyed 1,500 people in November 2024.

[2] *The 2025 Freeman Trust Report* shows brand trust fell to 71% in 2024, while trust in live events rose – 95% of attendees trust brands more after attending in-person. Available from www.freeman.com/resources/2025-freeman-trust-report/ [accessed 5 May 2025].

[3] *Freeman Trends Report* (2024).

[4] Marcie Merriman, *Is Gen Z the Spark We Need to See the Light?* (2021). Available from www.ey.com/en_us/insights/consulting/is-gen-z-the-spark-we-need-to-see-the-light-report [accessed 5 May 2025].

[5] Charlotte Tobitt, *Print Ad Revenue Halves in Six Years*, Press Gazette (22 February 2023). Available from https://pressgazette.co.uk/marketing/global-print-advertis ing-market-halves-in-six-years-but-publishers-struggling-to-compete-with-onl ine-oligopoly/ [accessed 5 May 2025].

[6] *The Freeman Trend Report 2024* states '68% of event organizers are at least moderately concerned about private events encroaching on their attendee and exhibitor pool.'

[7] Maybe the game is never over? The ESA, owners of E3, will launch a new gaming conference, iicon, in April 2026.

[8] Conversation, 2 December 2024.

[9] Founded in 2019, Hopin was the $7.75 billion virtual events Unicorn before selling event tech assets and handing back investor cash.

[10] Conversation, 19 February 2025.

[11] *The Chief Event Officer's Playbook* is focused on the power of live events, and there is no further detailed discussion of hybrid, except to say this. Every single live event now has some element of digital and content creation as part of it, whether that's streaming the mainstage or a more complex offering.

[12] Victor Frankl, *Man's Search for Meaning* (2008).
[13] Howard Bowen, *Social Responsibilities of the Businessman* (1953).
[14] United Nations, *Who Cares Wins Report* (2004).
[15] Global Reporting Initiative.
[16] Sustainability Standards Board.
[17] B. Joseph Pine II, *The Transformation Economy: Guiding Customers to Achieve Their Aspirations* (forthcoming).
[18] Experience delivered by Eat the Cake Studio.
[19] By Matt Middleton, John Swolfs and Matt Hougan.
[20] 'Meeting professionals expect internal meetings to the most frequent type.' AMEX GBT Meetings & Events 2025 Global Forecast.
[21] The global HVAC (cooling, heating and air ventilation industries) market size was estimated at US$249.37 billion in 2024 and is projected to grow at a CAGR of 7.5% from 2025 to 2030, according to Horizon Grand View Research, and has multiple association and commercial events.

Chapter 1

[1] Conversation, 30 January 2025.
[2] Conversation, 14 February 2025.
[3] Conversation, 15 April 2024.
[4] Conversation, 3 May 2024.
[5] Conversation, 31 January 2025.
[6] Conversation, 30 January 2025.
[7] Part of Informa, 2025's second largest ranking business media company in the UK after RELX. Bron Maher and Aisha Majid, *Press Gazette New Media Top 50 Ranking by Revenue* (January 2025). Available from https://pressgazette.co.uk/media_business/biggest-media-companies-uk-2025/ [accessed 5 May 2025].
[8] Stuart Lynch, *Diversity in Tech – Our Commitment* (2024). Available from https://mojdigital.blog.gov.uk/2024/02/13/diversity-in-tech-our-commitment/ [accessed 5 May 2025].
[9] This idea is explored further in Chapter 9.

Chapter 2

[1] Conversation, 18 April 2024.
[2] Joseph Campbell, *The Hero with a Thousand Faces* (1949).
[3] Joseph Pine, *Applying the Hero's Journey*, Substack (28 May 2024). Available from https://transformationsbook.substack.com/p/applying-the-heros-journey?utm_source=publication-search [accessed 5 May 2025].
[4] Robert McKee, *Story* (1999).
[5] By Ros Oxley.

[6] Christopher Booker, *The Seven Basic Plots: Why We Tell Stories* (2004).

[7] Professor Brian Cox Introduces COP26 (1 November 2021). Available from www.youtube.com/watch?v=PePS5ATi6d0 [accessed 5 May 2025].

[8] Email correspondence, 27 March 2025.

[9] Professor Mark Turner, *The Literary Mind* (1996). Available from https://markturner.org/lmx.html [accessed 5 May 2025].

[10] Donald Miller, *Building a StoryBrand* (2017).

[11] *The New York Times*, 30 July 2006.

[12] No matter the size or scale of your event, these principles still hold.

[13] Conversation with Alex Theuma, founder of SaaStock, 2 May 2025.

[14] *WPP Stream Yearbook* (2019).

[15] *The Freeman Trends Report 2024* research shows that 73% of attendees cite work or time pressures as non-attendance reasons.

[16] Conversation, 9 May 2024.

Chapter 3

[1] Jez Rose, LinkedIn post. Available from www.linkedin.com/posts/thatjezrose_conference-keynotespeaker-emcee-activity-7278804175528841217-89dy? [accessed 5 May 2025].

[2] *Gallup State of the Global Workplace Report* (2024).

[3] Deloitte's 2024 Gen Z and Millennial Survey connected with more than 22,800 respondents in 44 countries.

[4] By payments and fintech veterans from Google, TSYS and Citi.

[5] Conversation, 21 January 2025.

[6] Conversation, 16 April 2024.

[7] Sarah Bahr, Fyre Festival Ticket Holders Win $7,220 Each in Class-Action Settlement, *The New York Times* (15 April 2021). Available from www.nytimes.com/2021/04/15/arts/music/fyre-festival-settlement.html [accessed 5 May 2025].

[8] In February 2025, McFarland announced Fyre Festival 2 for 30 May 2025 off the coast of Cancún, Mexico. It was postponed in April 2025.

[9] Holly Edwards, BMJ, conversation, 28 January 2025.

[10] Conversation, 30 December 2024.

[11] On 17 April 2025.

[12] Conversation, 9 May 2024.

[13] *Bizzabo State of Events & Industry Benchmarks* (2025) surveyed 1,500 people in November 2024.

[14] World Travel Market, *Fueling the World with Travelpower!* Available from www.youtube.com/watch?v=UH3w31SfJ_U [accessed 5 May 2025].

Chapter 4

[1] Acquired in 2018 as part of the £3.9 billion acquisition of UBM.

[2] ICCA rankings 2023. Available from https://assets.simpleviewinc.com/simplev iew/image/upload/v1/clients/iccaweb/ICCA_Rankings_2023_230707_795d8 dd3-147a-45e2-b97f-075234e8f0f6.pdf [accessed 3 May 2025].

[3] International Congress and Convention Association, *Mobile World Congress Expects Economic Impact of €550 M and to Surpass Last Year's 101,000 Attendees* (May 2023). Available from https://barcelonacatalonia.eu/en/mobile-world-congress-expects-economic-impact-of-e550-m-and-to-surpass-last-years-101000-attendees/ [accessed 5 May 2025].

[4] Speak freely, but don't name names.

[5] Incisive Media sold its 'Insight' division, which included insurance and financial services publications, to Infopro Digital in March 2017.

[6] EIBTM was sold to Reed Exhibitions in 1997. IMEX launched in Frankfurt in 2003, and moved to Barcelona in 2004.

Chapter 5

[1] *Bizzabo State of Events and Industry Benchmarks* (2025).

[2] The delegate/sponsorship income balance varies according to your business model.

[3] A confex is a content-led event model combining a conference with a small exhibition.

[4] Conversation, 30 January 2025.

[5] Vivatech website. Available from https://vivatechnology.com/about [accessed 5 May 2025].

[6] Kate Moran, *The Four Dimensions of Tone of Voice* (August 2023). Available from www.nngroup.com/articles/tone-of-voice-dimensions/ [accessed 5 May 2025].

[7] Conversation, 30 January 2025.

[8] *Maritz Registration Insights Report April* (2024) analysed 360,000 attendee registration records over a three-year period.

Chapter 6

[1] *Amex GBT Meetings & Events 2025 Global Forecast*, surveyed 519 global meeting professionals. Available from https://experience.amexglobalbusinesstravel.com/me-forecast/2025/ [accessed 5 May 2025].

[2] New Scientist Live. Available from https://live.newscientist.com/ [accessed 5 May 2025].

³ Now owned by Daily Mail & General Trust under its Harmsworth Media Division, with a veritable who's who of media owners in its history since its founding by three science journalists in 1956.

⁴ Owned by The Stylist Group, a subsidiary of Scotland's DC Thomson.

⁵ Conversation, 9 April 2024.

⁶ The second largest trade show owner according STAX Research 2023. Available from www.tsnn.com/news/tsnn-exclusive-breaking-down-top-20-exhibition-org anizers-list [accessed 5 May 2025].

⁷ A concept from the world of theatre and TV, removing the invisible fourth wall between speaker and audience. See Chapter 7 for more discussion.

⁸ Conversation, 29 January 2025.

⁹ Conversation, 28 February 2025, author of *The Experience Economy* (1999) and The *Transformation Economy* (2026).

¹⁰ See Chapter 7 for more discussion of peak moments.

¹¹ Dame Steve Shirley, Why Do Ambitious Women Have Flat Heads? (March 2015). Available from www.ted.com/talks/dame_stephanie_shirley_why_do_ ambitious_women_have_flat_heads?language=en [accessed 5 May 2025].

¹² Email correspondence, 15 April 2024.

¹³ David Gray created the Empathy Map Canvas in 2010.

Chapter 7

¹ Largely emerging from J. Pine and J. Gilmore's, *The Experience Economy* (1999).

² Conversation, 10 February 2025.

³ J. Pine and J. Gilmore, *The Experience Economy* (1999).

⁴ Inspired by the work of celebrated artist and stage designer E.S. Devlin.

⁵ LinkedIn, *LinkedIn Is 'the place to B2B' at Cannes Lions 2024* (2024). Available from https://news.linkedin.com/2024/June/LinkedIn-is-the-place-to-B2B-at-Can nes-Lions-2024 [accessed 5 May 2025].

⁶ B. Joseph Pine II and James H. Gilmore, *The Experience Economy Competing for Customer Time, Attention, and Money* (1999, updated edition 2020).

⁷ B. Joseph Pine II, *The Transformation Economy: Guiding Customers to Achieve Their Aspirations* (forthcoming).

⁸ Joe Pine, *Chapter: Introduction to the Delta Model* (2024). Available from https:// transformationsbook.substack.com/p/chapter-introduction-to-the-delta?utm_ source=publication-search [accessed 5 May 2025].

⁹ Conversation, 28 February 2025.

¹⁰ Daniel Kahneman, *Thinking Fast and Slow*, 2011.

¹¹ Conversation, 1 August 2024.

¹² Conversation, 1 August 2024 as above, with Pigalle.

¹³ Conversation, 1 August 2024 as above, with Pigalle.

¹⁴ Conversation, 19 February 2025.

[15] The app is called SIX – more in Chapter 9.

[16] *The Value of Belonging at Work*, Betterup (2021). Available from https://grow. betterup.com/resources/the-value-of-belonging-at-work-the-business-case-for-investing-in-workplace-inclusion [accessed 5 May 2025].

[17] Conversation, 2 March 2025.

[18] Sarah Lkoepple, *Dreamforce 2022: Salesforce Went All Out to Celebrate the Event's 20th Anniversary*, BizBash (October 5 2022). Available from www.bizbash.com/production-strategy/event-production-fabrication/media-gallery/22484547/inside-salesforces-dreamforce-2022 [accessed 5 May 2025].

[19] LEGO set reference number: 624210 LEGO House 6 Bricks.

[20] Paul Zak, *How Extraordinary Experiences Create Happiness*, TedX Claremont Graduate University (2023). Available from www.youtube.com/watch?v=YlFC paJS0cE [accessed 5 May 2025].

[21] Chip and Dan Health, *The Power of Moments* (2017).

[22] STORIES – story, transformation, outside + offline, relationships, intensity, extraordinary and status + significance.

[23] Sold to Tarsus Group, later acquired by Informa.

[24] David Adler, *The Electric Magic of First Events: Why Now Is the Perfect Time to Start One*, Substack (17 February 2025). Available from https://substack.com/home/post/p-157343439 [accessed 5 May 2025].

[25] Constance Malleret, '*Like a Religious Thing*': *Free Lady Gaga Concert Draws 2.1m to Rio*, Guardian (4 May 2025). Available from www.theguardian.com/music/2025/may/04/like-a-religious-thing-free-lady-gaga-concert-draws-2-million-people-to-rio-de-janeiro-brazil?utm_source=chatgpt.com [accessed 5 May 2025].

[26] This event did not take place, due to the pandemic.

[27] Conversation, 20 February 2025.

Chapter 8

[1] Talk at the RSA, London, 17 June 2019.

[2] Conversation, 27 February 2025.

[3] Will Guidara, *Unreasonable Hospitality: The Remarkable Power of Giving People More Than They Expect* (2022).

[4] Will Guidara, *Unreasonable Hospitality* (2022), p. 80.

[5] *Virtual Worlds Forum Keynote* (October 2007). Podcast available from https://podcasts.apple.com/gb/podcast/virtual-worlds-forum-europe-2007-podcast/id26 0737834 [accessed 5 May 2025].

[6] In her insightful book, *The Art of Gathering* (2018), p. 177.

Chapter 9

[1] Conversation, 19 February 2025.

[2] Conversation, 3 February 2025.

[3] *LinkedIn B2B Marketing Benchmark: Regional Cut* (2023).

[4] Conversation, 25 February 2025.

[5] *Bizzabo State of Events & Industry Benchmarks* (2025) surveyed 1,500 people in November 2024.

[6] Conversation, 27 January 2025.

[7] *Bizzabo State of Events & Industry Benchmarks* (2025) surveyed 1,500 people in November 2024.

[8] *Outcomes from the UK Farm to Fork Summit.* Available from www.gov.uk/government/publications/outcomes-from-the-uk-farm-to-fork-sum mit and *PM sets out Blueprint to Boost British Fruit and Vegetable Sector: May 13 2024.* Available from www.gov.uk/government/news/pm-sets-out-blueprint-to-boost-british-fruit-and-vegetable-sector-may-13-2024 [accessed 5 May 2025].

[9] Conversation, 5 February 2025.

[10] *Tracking the Right Metrics for Event Success*, Biz Bash X Stova white paper (June 2024): 80.5%, followed by 45.3% social media monitoring, 34% on-site feedback stations and 23.1% focus groups.

[11] Shaping the Future of Events, ELX February 2025.

[12] Conversation, 5 February 2025.

[13] Julius Solaris, *Events Can't Be Measured is Over*, LinkedIn (August 2024). Available from www.linkedin.com/posts/juliussolaris_events-cant-be-measured-is-over-we-are-activity-7226229739235987457-m15e?utm_source=share&utm_medium=member_desktop&rcm=ACoAAACe3JIBneG_FN63Mff9x1XfeyKw3u9dBt4 [accessed 5 May 2025].

[14] Jack Phillips, M. Theresa Breining and Patricia Pulliam Philips, *Return on Investment in Meetings & Events* (2008).

[15] *Bizzabo State of Events and Industry Benchmarks* (2025).

[16] Accenture Strategy, *To Affinity and Beyond, From Me to We, the Rise of the Purpose-Led Brand* (2018).

[17] Fortuna Advisors and CEO Investor Forum, *The Return on Purpose: Before and during a Crisis* (2022).

[18] https://your6.com/.

[19] Conversation, 4 March 2025.

Chapter 10

[1] *Amex BT Meetings & Events 2025 Global Forecast.*

[2] *Bizzabo State of Events & Industry Benchmarks* (2025), surveyed 1500 people in November 2024.

[3] One global head of corporate events told me, 'I'm talking directly to my manager's manager, I'm on the radar of the C-level execs, because I've earned the respect. I have the equity.'

[4] 67% of marketing leaders are increasing budgets for brand-building efforts, LinkedIn B2B Marketing Benchmark, The B2B Marketing Organization of Tomorrow, 2024.

[5] The Power of Events, Support Organisation Profile. Available from www.thepo werofevents.org/industry-community/support-organisations/events-apprenti ceships/ [accessed 5 May 2025].

[6] Sam Altman, CEO of OpenAI, *The Logan Bartlett Show Interview* (14 May 2024). Available from https://www.theloganbartlettshow.com/archive/ep-104-sam-alt man-talks-gpt-4o-and-predicts-the-future-of-ai [accessed 5 May 2025].

Bibliography

Transformation, journey and purpose

Christopher Booker (2004) *Seven Basic Plots*. Continuum.

Joseph Campbell (2008) *The Hero with a Thousand Faces*. New World Library.

Viktor Frankl (2008) *Man's Search for Meaning*. Rider.

Margaret Kerrison (2022) *Immersive Storytelling*. Michael Wiese Productions.

Robert McKee (1998) *Story*. Methuen.

Priya Parker (2019) *The Art of Gathering: How We Meet and Why It Matters*. Penguin.

B. Joseph Pine II (forthcoming) *The Transformation Economy*. Harvard Business Review Press.

Simon Sinek (2009) *Start With Why*. Penguin Business.

Christopher Vogler (2007, 2020) *The Writers Journey: Mythic Structures for Writers*. Michael Wiese Productions.

Messaging, content and experience

Roel Frissen, Ruud Janssen and Dennis Luijer (2016) *Event Design Handbook*. BIS.

Seth Godin (2018) *This Is Marketing*. Penguin Business.

Nick Gold (2020) *Speak with Conference*. Penguin.

Chip and Dan Heath (2017) *The Power of Moments*. Bantam Press.

Gary Klein (2013) *Seeing What Others Don't*. Oxford.

Matthew Lieberman (2015) *Social: Why Our Brains Are Wired to Connect*. Oxford University Press.

Susan Magsamen and Ivy Ross (2023) *Your Brain on Art: How the Arts Transform Us*. Canongate Books.

Donald Miller (2017) *Building a StoryBrand*. Harper Collins Leadership.

David Ogilvy (1995) *Ogilvy on Advertising*. Welbeck Publishing Group.

B. Joseph Pine II and James H Gilmore (1999) *The Experience Economy*. Harvard Business Review Press.

J. Robert Rossman and Matthew D. Duerden (2019) *Designing Experiences*. Columbia University Press.

Pigalle Tavakkolli (2025) *The Experience Design Building Blocks*. School of Experience Design.

James Wallman (2019) *Time and How to Spend It*. Penguin.

Paul Zak (2023) *Immersion: The Science of the Extraordinary and the Source of Happiness*. Lioncrest Publishing.

Welcome and outcomes

Chris Anderson (2024) *Infectious Generosity*. W.H. Allen.

Tahira Endean (2025) *Our KPI Is Joy*. Independent.

Will Guidara (2022) *Unreasonable Hospitality*. Ebury Edge.

Jack Phillips, M. Theresa Breining and Patricia Pulliam Philips (2008) *Return on Investment in Meetings & Events*. Butterworth-Heinemann.

Index

A

abandoned cart rate 124
ACP funnel 121
Adler, David 178
Adobe Summit 88, 95
Advertising Week 33, 125
advisory boards 158
Aggarwal, Anil 61, 149
Allen, Samme 172–173
Altman, Sam 220
Angelou, Maya 168
Animal Health Event 86
Anthropy Conference
        10–11
art 37–38, 174–175
Artificial Intelligence 2–3,
        17, 34, 71, 76, 87,
        95, 133, 170, 192,
        198, 218
associations,
        transformational
        events in 17
audience
    attention 13, 37, 46, 49,
        50, 56–57, 71, 116,
        138, 142, 153, 162,
        173, 179
    authentic selves of
        112–113
    curation 104, 105, 106–
        110, 113
    engagement of 61, 73,
        75–76
    significance of 10
    types 90–91, 105–106,
        111–112
Audience Curation Grid
        109
authenticity 3–6, 36,
        112–113
automations 2, 9, 11, 124,
        187

B

B Corp movement 61
B2B Rocks conference 55
Badge Question Box
        147–148
Bailey, Oli 213

Bain & Company 209
Barcelona 88, 174, 185
Barrett, Felix 172
Battelle, John 32, 56, 74
belonging, hardwiring
        into experience
        170–171
Bidamant, Mathieu 217
birds of a feather sessions
        147
Bisconti, Colleen 208
Bizzabo 206
Blank, Steve 73
Bloom, Ray 92
Bloomberg House 139
board-level conversation
        219–220
Bodgan-Martin, Doreen
        192, 198
Booker, Christopher 47
B-Positive Choir 174
Braindates 148
brand
    development 115–116
    experiences 46, 165
    marketing 70–71, 73
breaking the fourth wall
        146, 173–174
Breakthru Meeting
        Programme 149
British Medical Journal
        (BMJ) 68–69,
        175
British Small Animal
        Veterinary
        Association
        Congress 168
British Society of
        Haematology 174
broken model question
        9–11
Brown, Brené 207, 214
Brownlee, Neil 181
business models 8–9, 17,
        50, 91, 97
business objectives 149,
        217, 220
Business of Opera, The 195,
        197

Butcher, Andrew 54
buy side 90, 94–95, 97, 99;
        see also delegates
        (buy side)

C

Call for Papers model
        152–153
call to adventure 46, 53–54,
        220
Campbell, Joseph 44–45,
        220
campfires 146
Cannes Lions International
        Festival of
        Creativity 165
Canva Create 76–77
Caravan Camping &
        Motorhome Show
        149–150
celebration (5Cs model)
        15
ceremony (5Cs model) 15
Chief Marketing Officer
        (CMO) 18, 75, 219,
        220
Chief Purpose Officer 13,
        14, 60
Chief Vision Officer 13,
        14, 60
Claims Club 92
Clarke, Paul 129–130
Cleaver, Eldridge 46
climate change issues
        12–13, 69–70
Club Ichi 74
Coetzee, Helen 121
cold open theory 196–197
collective effervescence 179
combat designers, video
        game 84
Comic-Con 185
Comicon, MCM 87
communications strategy
        127–129
community 15
    author's background 6–7
    belonging and meaning
        219

building 67, 69, 74–75, 134, 137, 170, 218
ecosystem understanding 7–8
competitors analysis 56–58
connection (5Cs model) 14
connection gatherings 74, 144
consultative sales 125–126
contamination stories 48
content
  bringing organization's story to life 136–138
  committees 157–158
  curation principles 138–139
  definition and importance 133–134, 140–141
  event design 135–136, 153–154
  hard content 144, 145–147
  as market driver 85
  plan 158–159
  research strategies 150–153
  soft content 144, 147–148
  soft social networking 144, 148–150
  and speakers/talent recruitment 154–157
  specific provocation 141–142
  strategy 144–145
  themes 142–144
content (5Cs model) 14
content design 162, 183, 191
Content Flat Plan 159
content marketing 54, 101, 116–117, 218
content-led content marketing strategy 117
corporate events 16–17, 78, 93, 95; see also organizational events
corporate social responsibility (CSR) 13–14, 61
cosy corners 147
Cottrell-Boyce, Frank 206
Covey, Stephen 38

Cox, Brian 48–49
Craig, Claire 26–27
Creative Open 194, 195
Crellin, Naomi Clare 171
Criado-Perez, Caroline 130
customer lifetime value 210
customer service 205

D
Daisley, Bruce 142
data
  utilization 118
  visualization 88–89
Davis, Tessa 188
De Esteban, Max 37–38
delegates (buy side) 59, 90–91, 93–94, 96–97, 99, 100, 106, 120
Deloitte 141
dementia research 29–30
design principles 161, 216
design thinking principles 158–159
DFTB (Don't Forget the Bubbles) 180, 188
Didion, Joan 49
differentiators 57–58
digital channels 4, 8, 11, 12
Dreamforce 176–177
drinks, networking 148
Dunbar's number 191
Dundee, Scotland 180–181
Duolingo 114
Durkheim, Émile 179
Dyball, Jane 28

E
E3 (Electronic Entertainment Expo) 9–10
Edwards, Holly 68
EE Home Presents: The Circus 172
80/20 rule, of content marketing 116
elevation theory 178
email marketing 118
emotion design 168–170
emotional engagement 5, 44, 46–47
Empathy Map 159
employee engagement 61, 78
Endean, Tahira 213
environmental, social, and governance (ESG) 13, 61, 71

European Society of Cardiology Congress 208
EURORDIS 74
EuroTier trade fair (Deutsche Landwirtschafts-Gesellschaft) 86–87
Event Brand Guide 115–116
Event Differentiator Checklist 58
Event Evolution Model 4, 26, 44
Event Ikigai Worksheet 68
Event Market Competitor Template 58
event marketing 39, 73, 79; see also market mapping
  funnel model 120–121
  power and challenges of 105
event markets 84–86, 89–90
Event Participant Hero's Journey 46
Event Purpose Proposition 37, 41–42, 58, 75–76, 79, 83, 102, 103–105, 116, 122, 126, 128, 184, 197, 203
event strategy 75, 79, 216, 217, 219
event tech stack 11, 12
event value equation 57
event-led strategy 117
Everyman Cinema 196
experience design 5, 104, 149, 160, 161–163, 169, 176, 181, 183, 190
  and art 174–175
  and belonging 170–171
  breaking the fourth wall 173–174
  emotion design 168–170
  experience economy 163–166
  happiness and love 177–178
  immersive experiences 171–173
  levels of experiences 166–167
  memorable moments 178–179
  placemaking 180–181

and play 175
   surprise and delight
      elements 176–177
   transformation economy
      166–167
Experience Profiles 171
EY 4
Eyth, Max 86
Ezekiel, Laurent 146

F
Farm to Fork Summits
   206–207
feedback 151, 159, 205, 207,
   208, 224
festivalization 163, 172
fidget and skill toys 175
FIFDH (Geneva
   International Film
   Festival on Human
   Rights) 214
financial health advocacy
   71
financial markets 94–95
fireside chats 145
firewalks 179
fishbowls 146
5Cs model 14–16
Fleabag 173
FOMO (fear of missing
   out) 123
Forster, Debbie 35
Foundling Museum 180
FT's Global Banking
   Summit 71, 73
Future Proof Festival
   15–16, 149
Fyre Festival 65

G
G8 Summit 2005 47–48
game development events
   84–85
Gathering Story Pillars
   54, 59
Gawande, Atul 130
Geldof, Sir Bob 47
generational differences
   4–5, 13, 61, 74
Gill, Gina 63
Gilmore, James 163, 165–
   166, 167
Gilmore, Leigh 139
Gingrich, Newt 53
Giussani, Bruno 69–70
Gladwell, Malcolm 191
Global Fashion Summit
   143

Gold, Nick 204
Golden Circle framework
   62
Goodwood events 162–163
Goodwoof 163
Google DeepMind 34
government events 17, 206
GovTech Summit 63, 76
Great Ormond Street
   Children's
   Hospital (GOSH)
   51
Green, Martin, CBE 43–44,
   53
Green, Will 56
Groupe Les Echos 112
Guerilla Science 169
Guglani, Sam 64
Guidara, Will 189, 190

H
hackathons 25, 146
happiness 169, 177–178
hard content 144, 145–147
Hassabis, Demis 34
headteacher's conference
   202–203
Heath, Chip and Dan 178
hero's journey 44–46,
   50–51, 220
HLTH conference 167
hospitality 189, 190, 196,
   223
hosted buyer model 92
Hull UK City of Culture
   2017 43–44, 53
hybrid events 12

I
IBC Legal Studies
   Employment Law
   Update 25
IBTM Barcelona 116
IBTM World 143, 185
ikigai
   personal model 66–67
   professional model
      67–70
IMEX 92, 116, 213
Immersion Neuroscience
   170–171, 213
immersive experiences 12,
   44, 171–173, 181
Impact Days 214
impact measurement
   206–214
individual transformation
   27, 29–30

influencers 7, 65, 119
information management
   2–3
Inhouse Farming
   Event 86
In-Housing Summit
   (Campaign) 34
in-housing trend 34–35
in-person experience 4, 6, 9,
   12, 14
Insurance Post Magazine
   91
Intergalactic Travel Bureau,
   Guerilla Science
   169
International Confex 116
International Congress
   of Parkinson's
   Disease and
   Movement
   Disorders 147
International Food and
   Drink Event (IFE)
   87
International MICE
   Summit 31–32
ISE (Integrated Systems
   Europe) 174
ITU (International
   Telecoms Union)
   192, 198

J
Jobs, Steve 49, 150
Journal House (*Wall Street
   Journal*) 165
journey, of participants
   41–42, 183,
   215–216
benchmarking 56–57
call to adventure 53–54
consolidation of
   narrative 58
contextualization 55–56
crafting of 54
differentiators,
   articulation of
   57–58
Hull City of Culture
   example 43–44
narrative identity 48–49
narrative models 44–48
participants as heroes
   52
and Transformative
   Journey Plan
   49–51
visualization 42

K

Kahneman, Daniel 168
Kastner, Nicola 201
Kean, Amy 142
Key Performance
    Indicators (KPIs)
    204, 210
keynotes and presentations
    145
Kidzania 163
Kilkenomics festival 72, 76

L

Lady Gaga concert 179
Laidlaw Opera Trust 194,
    197
Lanyard colours 148
Lathan, Liz 74
lead times 120, 122–123
leadership inspiration
    62–63
Lego House 164, 177,
    189
lightning talks 145
Lincoln, Abraham 39
Linney, Piers 10–11
Live 8 concerts 47
live events 5–6, 8, 140, 197,
    213, 219
live polling 147
Livingston, Gill 29–30
London Conference 114
London Motor Show 162
London Tech Week 33–34
Love Plus philosophy
    177–178

M

Magic Castle Hotel 178
Magsamen, Susan 174
Maguire, Kevin 142
Manningham-Buller,
    Baroness Eliza
    173–174
Marantz, Jason 202–203
March, Lord 162
Mariano Joaquim,
    Bernardo, Junior
    24–25
market
    definition of 87–88
    market flow 85–87
    market makers 94–95
    research strategies
        151–152
market mapping 103, 104,
    105, 119, 183, 184

articulation of market's
    drivers with 91–93
benefits of 89–90
building engagement
    and leveraging
    value 101–102
as communication tool
    89
four core quadrants
    90–91
inclusions 99–101
principles 90–91
and purpose 102
as superpower 90
template 96
uniqueness of market 99
workshop process 96–99
marketing channels 1, 75,
    101, 121, 209, 219
marketing effectiveness 209
Marketing Loop 121, 123
marketing straplines 70–71
Mask, Clate 49–50
Master of Ceremonies
    (MC) 195–196
Mattiassich-Aszody, Eszter
    129
Maws, Marjorie 52, 223
Máxima, Queen of the
    Netherlands 71
Mayer, Catherine 28–29
McAdams, Dan 48
McCandless, David 88–89
McFarland, Billy 65
McKee, Robert 46
McWilliams, David 72, 76
measurement see
    transformation
    outcome
    evaluation
    (measurement)
media and press 98–99, 106
media partnerships
    119–120
media reach, evaluation
    of 212
media-owned events 17
messaging 127–129
Medicine Unboxed 64
memorable moments 44,
    130, 153, 162, 169,
    178–179
messaging 104–105, 183,
    190
audience types 105–106
brand development
    115–116

communication
    community
    127–128
communication strategy
    128–130
consultative vs
    commodity sales
    approach 125–
    126
consumer brands,
    learning from
    123–124
content marketing
    116–117
core messages, audience-
    based 110–115
funnels and loops
    120–11
lead times 122
and long-term
    partnerships 126
marketing partnerships
    122
multi-channel
    marketing strategy
    117–120
Participant Persona
    Messaging Grid
    113–114
shorter event horizons
    123
sponsor storytelling
    124–125
and third-party events
    126–127
Meyer, Nico 175
MICE industry 143
Microsoft events 10–11
Miller, Donald 50–51
Mobile World Congress
    (MWC) 88
Money 20/20 61–62
Moore, Alan 52, 150
Mordaunt, Penny 154
Mortimer, Ruth 33, 111
movement, sector
    transformation
    as 36
MPI European Conference
    172–173
Murdoch, Rupert 53
museums, sensor
    monitoring in
    37–38
must-haves quadrant
    90–91, 98, 129; see
    also VIPs

N

Nambatingué, Nata 208
narrative models 54
    application of 50–51
    fear and greed factors
        46–47
    hero's journey 44–46
    narrative identity 48–49
    power of 44
    seven basic plots 47–48
Nathan, Rob 162
National Bed Federation
    (NBF) 94
National Caravan Council
    (NCC) 149–150
neglected open source
    tools 25
Neilson Norman Group
    115
nemawashi process 127
Net Promoter Score (NPS)
    209–210
Netflix 12, 65, 125, 165
networking 148–149
neuroaesthetics 174
Neves, Miguel 31
New Scientist Live 136
New Yorker app 176
News Corporation
    conference 53–54
Next Gen Event Goers
    (NGEG) 4, 121

O

O'Brien, John 11
Odom, George 210
offer-led strategy 117
Office, The (television) 197
Oles, Erin 176
online events 11, 12
Open Data Institute (ODI)
    130, 141–142
Open Source Program
    Offices 25
Open Source Week, UN 25
organizational success
    217–218
organizational
    transformation
    27–28, 30–32
Osibodu, Nicole 74
Oxley, Ros 93–94, 223
oxytocin 170

P

paid media 118–119
pandemic acceleration
    11–12

panels 145
Parker, Priya 187, 196
Parry, Adam 135
participant experience 60,
    64, 67–68
Participant Persona
    Messaging Grid
    113–114
Pavoni, Silvia 71
Peak End Rule 159
peak experiences 178–179
Pebble Beach event (2006)
    53
Pechakucha/Ignite talks 145
Pension Funds Mission
    (UK) 95
Personal Ikigai Worksheet
    66, 67
P&G Signal Summit 32
PHD UK, 'Is Optimism
    Dead?' event 142
Phillips ROI
    Methodology™
    210
photography and
    videography
    128–130
PhotoVogue Festival
    (Vogue) 143
Pine, Joseph 13, 46, 151,
    163, 165–167
Pixar 49
Place to B2B, The
    (LinkedIn) 165
placemaking 180–181
play, power of 175
pop-up models 33, 74, 169
PPC (pay per click)
    118–119
pricing models 117,
    123–124
Primadonna Festival 28
print ad revenue model 8
Pritchard, Marc 32
product, event as 5
programme committees
    157–158
Punchdrunk theatre 172
purpose 24–25, 59–60,
    183, 184, 192, 193,
    216–217
    articulating the power
        of 79
    community and
        connection 74
    and event strategies 75
    in events 71–72
    failure of promise 65

generational need 60–62
Ikigai 66–70
knowing your purpose
    60
and market mapping 102
and marketing straplines
    70–71
and marketing value
    propositions 73
proposition 75–78
purpose-driven events/
    work 13–14,
    16–17, 61
why model 62–64
Purpose Evaluation Plan 38

Q

Queen's Women Network
    26–27

R

RainFocus Insight 2025
    171
Rank, Otto 44
Reading Rights Summit
    206
redemptive stories 48–49
Reed Exhibitions 87
registration optimization
    123–124
remote work, and internal
    events 16
Return on Experience
    (ROE/ROX) 211
Return on Investment
    (ROI) 204,
    210–211
Return on Purpose 211
Return on Relationships
    (ROR) 211–212
Richardson, Chloe 204
Richmond Events 92
Ridzon, Lynn 210
Risky Business conference
    51
Robbins, Tony 179
Roosegaarde, Daan 173
Roosevelt, Eleanor 141
Rose, Jez 60
Ross, Ivy 174
Rowan, David 211–212
Rowley, Phil 142

S

Saarinen, Eero 161
Saarinen, Eliel 161, 216
SaaS (Software as a Service)
    events 55–56

sale messages 125
Salesforce 55
Scholar, Debi 210
Secret Cinema 172
sector transformation 32–36
Seitler, Moses 78
sell side 90, 94–95, 97–98, 99, 124; *see also* sponsors and exhibitors (sell side)
SEO (Search Engine Optimization) 120
serendipity 135, 149
service, event as 5
Sharpe, Fay 204, 207
Shirley, Dame Steve 155–156
Shoptalk 149
Simmons, Dame Melinda 47–48
Sinek, Simon 62–63
single source of truth 102, 116
Sissay, Lemn 202–203
SIX app 213
social media 56, 105, 115, 119, 138, 175
soft content 144, 147–148
soft social networking 144, 148–149
Solaris, Julius 208
speaker recruitment 154–157
speed-dating 148
sponsors and exhibitors (sell side) 90–91, 94, 97–98, 106
messaging 124–127
sponsor storytelling 124–125
sponsor-led events 91
stakeholders 83–84; *see also* market; market mapping
Starbucks 163
Strong Woman 137
STORIES framework 178
Story Grid 103
Story Pillars 105, 116
StoryBooks (TISE) 52
StoryBrand Framework 50–51
Storycraft Lab 171
storytelling *see* narrative model

Strategic Meetings Management (SMM) 210
strategic value 202, 217
strategy, significance of 10, 18–19, 23–24
Stylist Live 137
Stylist magazine 136–137
surprise and delight elements 176–177
surveys 152, 158, 205, 208
sustainability 12–13
Swift, Taylor 74
SXSW London 152–153
System 1 and System 2 thinking 168

T
Tavakkoli, Pigalle 168–169
team collaboration 38–39, 42
Tech Nation data 35
Tech Show London (Closer Still Media) 95
Tech Talent Charter 35–36
tech-enabled short double opt-in meetings 148
technology, real-time analysis 212
technology impact 11–12
TED Countdown 69–70
TED talks 156, 214
thank you practices 156–157
themed tables 147
themes 142–144
third-party events 126–127
This Day Thank You event 78
TISE (The International Surface Event), Informa 52
tone of voice 114–115, 119, 124, 187
Trade Missions 95
trade shows and conferences 17, 93
transformation 23–24, 44, 151, 183, 184, 192, 216, 217, 219
aim of 26–27
event as 5
and journey 42
overarching questions 36–37
and purpose 24–26

and team collaboration 38–39, 42
vision 37–38
transformation categories 27–29
individual focus 27, 29–30
organizational focus 27–28, 30–32
sector focus 28, 32–36
Transformation Categories Grid 37, 102
transformation economy 166–167
Transformation Journey Plan 49–51, 59, 79, 102
transformation outcome evaluation (measurement) 201–203
as an initial strategy 205–206
bigger impact 213–214
challenges 204
data collection process 205
effectiveness of 203–204
event impact and legacy 207–208
items to measure 208–209
long-term impact 206–207
models 209–212
technology and strategy 213
through media reach 212
trust building 2–6, 138
Turner, Mark 50
Turrell, Mark 72

U
unconferences 146
unDavos 72
unique narrative proposition (UNP) 55
unique selling proposition (USP) 55

V
V&A Dundee 181
value propositions 73–75
Van Mellaerts, Julien 195
Video Challenge 147

video game industry events 84–85
VIPs 106
  messaging 127
  VIP Invitation List 98
virtual events 12
Virtual Worlds Forum 128, 188, 191
visitor promotion (visprom) 87, 95
visualization 88–90
VivaTech 111–112, 114
VOYAGERS 211–212

W
Wallman, James 178
Washington International Spy Museum 163–164
Web Summit 135
webinars 14, 25, 84
websites 117–118
Weiner, Jonathan 61, 167

welcome 183–184
  cinema experience, learning from 196
  and closing, link between 197
  cold open 196–197
  contextual 188
  easy 188–189
  engagement upfront 194–195
  generous 189–190
  hard 191
  journey design 193–194
  MCs and stageless welcomes 195–196
  opening words 192–193
  pre-welcome welcome 187–188
  at scale 191–192
  significance of 184–185
  soft 190
  warm welcome 185–187

Welcome Conference, The 190
Welcome Planning Grid 194
Workshop, Market Map 96–99
workshops 145
World Café format 147
World Economic Forum 72, 139, 143–144
World Experience Summit 178
World Travel Market (WTM) (RX Global) 77
WPP Stream conference 146

Z
Zak, Paul 12, 170–171, 177–178, 201, 213
Zibrant 207